A Practical Guide to Insolvency

kavanaghfennell⌘

D1637498

Chartered
Accountants
Ireland

Published by
Chartered Accountants Ireland
Chartered Accountants House
47–49 Pearse Street
Dublin 2
www.charteredaccountants.ie

© Chartered Accountants Ireland 2009

This publication is designed to provide accurate and authoritative information in regard to the subject matter covered. It is provided on the understanding that Chartered Accountants Ireland is not engaged in rendering professional services. If professional advice or other expert assistance is required, the services of a competent professional should be sought.

ISBN 978-0-903854-92-4

Typeset by Typeform, Dublin
Printed by ColourBooks, Dublin, Ireland

CHAPTER 6 continued..

CHAPTER 7 Investigations

CHAPTER 8 Advising a Client in Financial Difficulty: Consensual Restructuring and Enforced Solutions

CHAPTER 8 continued..

CHAPTER 9   Relevant Parties

First, I wish to acknowledge the foresight and vision of Michael Diviney and Chartered Accountants Ireland who planted the seed for the writing of this book.

Secondly, I would like to acknowledge the dedication and hard work of a special team of people from Kavanagh Fennell for assisting me in organising and collating all the content and information for this book. Michael Leydon led the project with vigour and incredible attention to detail, and Ken Tyrrell provided invaluable insight into the structure, format and layout.

The book would not have been possible without the hard work of Andrew Byrne, James Anderson, Colm Fitzpatrick, Mark Degnan, Colin Gaynor, Eoin Healy and Marie McCaffrey who drafted the 'meat and bones' of the various chapters.

This book is a tribute to my partners Ken Fennell and David Van Dessel and the whole team at Kavanagh Fennell who over the years have developed the knowledge and know-how that is shared in these pages.

To them I am deeply grateful.

Tom Kavanagh, FCA

Chapter >> 1

Introduction

Chapter 1 Overview

Introduction

Since the first signs of the economic downturn in the latter stages of 2006, interest in the area of insolvency has increased significantly. This specialist area of the accounting profession had been largely forgotten in Ireland for the 12-year period from 1995 to early 2007. The boom years, with record growth levels, saw insolvencies slow to a trickle relative to the level of economic activity.

However, since the first quarter of 2007, as the impact of the downturn truly emerged, there has been a dramatic increase in the level of, and interest in, formal insolvencies and the whole area of restructuring and turnarounds.

The purpose of this book is simple. It is designed to be a desktop manual for business people in general on the basics of insolvency. It will be a valuable tool for accountants in practice and/or in industry, for solicitors, trading companies, bankers, credit controllers, business managers and other professionals.

This book explains:

- the various types of insolvency in easy to understand layman's terms;

- the thinking behind each type; and

- the circumstances where each is most appropriate.

The book will be helpful in formulating a strategy for the reader, whether the reader's business is in financial difficulty or whether the reader is an advisor, creditor, debtor, insurer or in any way affected by a company in financial difficulty.

 Recent History

The 1980s recession was a busy time for insolvency professionals. All the leading, what was then 'Big 6', accounting firms had large insolvency divisions. At this time although a lot of the smaller cases were done by smaller professional firms, there was a substantial amount of large receivership work, which in the main went to the Big 6.

In 1990, companies legislation, and in particular the provisions relating to insolvency, were substantially updated for the first time since 1963 with the introduction of the Companies Act 1990. That year also saw, as a result of the Goodman collapse, the advent of examination legislation, and this added a significant new tool for insolvency practitioners in their efforts to save trading businesses.

The history of corporate insolvency since the enactment of the Companies Act 1990 makes interesting reading, and is outlined in the Table on page 4.

As would be expected, during the boom years of 1995–2006, receivership work declined in general and most insolvencies arose as creditors' voluntary liquidations "CVLs" or court liquidations.

Insolvencies in Ireland: 1990-2009

YEAR	CVL	Court Liquidations	Receiverships	Examinerships	Total
1990	439	62	96	45	**642**
1991	538	52	77	21	**688**
1992	254	83	139	36	**512**
1993	443	62	113	3	**621**
1994	580	38	77	23	**718**
1995	494	34	53	8	**589**
1996	552	36	31	13	**632**
1997	404	29	33	13	**479**
1998	361	49	27	13	**450**
1999	315	22	11	1	**349**
2000	324	32	27	2	**385**
2001	415	24	21	9	**469**
2002	378	34	38	12	**462**
2003	346	31	36	11	**424**
2004	321	40	18	6	**385**
2005	300	49	19	4	**372**
2006	323	31	17	3	**374**
2007	308	36	14	21	**379**
2008	530	83	59	49	**721**
2009 (Eight Months)	744	88	105	48	**985**

Statistics courtesy of www.insolvencyjournal.ie; and Tom McGovern, Companies Registration Office

The total number of Insolvencies in 1990 was 642, and remained in or around this level until 1997 when the level dropped below 500. By 1999, the number had fallen below 400.

In the early part of the new millennium, insolvency levels increased again due to the impact of international events such as the outbreak of foot and mouth disease, the Dotcom Bust, the collapse of Enron and the terrorist assault on the Twin Towers on 11 September 2001. By 2004, however, the numbers were again declining and remained below 400 until the end of 2007.

It was during the latter stages of 2008 that the full extent of the downturn became clear with the figure for insolvencies almost doubling to 721. By the end of the second quarter of 2009, there had already been 703 insolvencies and at present, the prediction for 2009 remains in excess of 1,200.

Readers are referred to www.insolvencyjournal.ie, which produces regular updates on statistics and insolvency notices (creditors' meetings, judgements and petitions) across the country.

 Developments in Irish Insolvency

Other than the substantial changes in the number of insolvencies, there have been significant changes in how the market is serviced by the accounting firms. Since 1990, there has been a notable emergence of practices offering specialist insolvency services including Kavanagh Fennell.

Another very significant development in Irish insolvency was the establishment of the Office of the Director of Corporate Enforcement in 2001.

This has been a key catalyst for the improvement in the behaviour of directors in recent years and forces an important discipline on liquidators to prepare a comprehensive report on the behaviour of a director in a court or creditors' voluntary liquidation.

Due to Globalisation and the many multinationals operating in Ireland the European Union, Uncitral and cross-border insolvencies feature more prominently than ever in Irish insolvency as Europe faces unprecedented times of financial uncertainty. Interestingly, while insolvencies have increased across the European Union, very few countries have seen the sheer level of percentage increases in insolvencies as Ireland.

Potentially, the largest development in Irish insolvency in recent times is the reaction of the Irish government to the financial difficulties in the Irish banking system and the resulting creation of the National Asset Management Agency or "NAMA". NAMA will look to take certain potentially toxic assets and the associated non-performing loans to shore up the balance sheets of many Irish banks and restore stability to the banking sector. At the time of writing, the legislation has yet to be enacted and the impact of NAMA remains a subject of considerable debate.

In relation to personal insolvency, there has been no change in any of the legal bankruptcy procedures, which are now clearly outdated for the needs of the modern economy.

During the recent boom there has been substantial lending to individuals who now face considerable financial difficulty. Changes in the level of debt needed to place a person into bankruptcy are expected in the near future. However, the need for a new direction on personal insolvency is very evident. As a result of the punitive nature of the present bankruptcy legislation, the numbers of bankrupts (10 to the end of June 2009) and arranging debtors (six to the end of June 2009) remain illogically low when compared to corporate statistics and those of many other European jurisdictions (statistics courtesy of Barry O'Neill, Eugene F. Collins, Solicitors).

Despite a lot of discussion regarding the licensing of insolvency practitioners, there is still no requirement to hold a licence to practice in insolvency in Ireland. This differs from the applicable rules in Britain and Northern Ireland. However, it must be expected that eventually licensing will too be required to practice as an Insolvency Practitioner in this jurisdiction.

 **Conclusion**

It is at present difficult to see when the current financial difficulties facing Ireland will end. Insolvency levels are unprecedented and considerable uncertainty remains as regards the country's banking system, the country's key developers and the legislative reaction to same.

Given the financial times we currently face, we have no doubt that you will find this book of use and benefit in the coming months and years.

The reader can also benefit from the introduction of a new Diploma in Insolvency by Chartered Accountants Ireland and planned seminars on insolvency in the near future.

Chapter ▶▶ 2

Creditors' Voluntary
Liquidations

Chapter 2 Overview

▶▶ What is a creditors' voluntary liquidation?

▶▶ Legislation, and guidance from Chartered Accountants Ireland

▶▶ When is a creditors' voluntary liquidation suitable/appropriate?

▶▶ Who are the key parties involved?

▶▶ Recent statistics

▶▶ The process involved in a creditors' voluntary liquidation

▶▶ Planning the meetings of members and creditors

▶▶ The meeting of members (shareholders)

▶▶ The meeting of creditors

▶▶ The Committee of Inspection

▶▶ Following the conclusion of the meeting

▶▶ The liquidator's role and function

▶▶ Investigations

▶▶ Closing a creditors' voluntary liquidation

▶▶ Case study: *Tralee Beef and Lamb Limited*

▶▶ Frequently Asked Questions

What is a creditors' voluntary liquidation?

A creditors' voluntary liquidation (CVL) is a process whereby:

- a liquidator is appointed to an insolvent company;

- its affairs are investigated;

- its assets are realised;

- creditors are paid in a strict legal preference; and ultimately

- the company is legally dissolved.

Legislation, and guidance from Chartered Accountants Ireland

The main legislative provisions concerning liquidators are set out in the following:

- Part VI of the Companies Act 1963 (CA 1963)

- Part VI of the Companies Act 1990 (CA 1990)

- Part 5 of the Company Law Enforcement Act 2001 (CLEA 2001).

Statements of Insolvency Practice are issued by Chartered Accountants Ireland to insolvency practitioners with a view to maintaining standards by setting out

required practice and harmonising the approach of members to particular aspects of insolvency. The purpose of the Statements of Insolvency Practice is to set out basic principles and essential procedures with which insolvency practitioners are required to comply. In terms of creditors' voluntary liquidation, the following Statements of Insolvency Practice (SIPs) are of relevance:

- S191208: Anti-money Laundering for Insolvency Practitioners

- S2B: Liquidator's Investigation into the Affairs of an Insolvent Company

- S7B: Preparation of Receipts And Payments

- S8B: Planning and Administration of Creditors' Meetings

- S9B: Remuneration of insolvency officeholders

- S10B: Proxy Forms

- S11B: The Handling Of Funds

- S13B: Acquisition of assets of insolvent companies

- S15B: Dealing with employee claims

- S17B: Committee of Inspection

- S18B: Reporting by Liquidators

When is a creditors' voluntary liquidation suitable/appropriate?

The creditor's voluntary liquidation process is the most common form of insolvency in Ireland and is predominantly used in the following circumstances:

- the company is no longer in a position to pay its debts as they fall due

- the company's financial position and/or asset position is likely to deteriorate further

- the financial position of the company's creditors (individually or as a whole) will be worsened by the company's continued trading

- the company's business is no longer viable

- a restructuring of debt is not possible

- a receivership has ended and the company's affairs are to be closed off and the company legally dissolved.

 ## Who are the key parties involved?

The process of placing a company into liquidation is discussed in detail below. However, the main parties involved in the process are as follows:

- **The Company's Directors**
  The directors instigate the process by calling meetings of members and creditors. A director of the company must also preside at these meetings as chairperson of same.

- **The Company's Shareholders**
  At the meeting of shareholders, the shareholders will consider the company's solvency and consider/ appoint a liquidator.

- **The Company's Creditors**
  At the meeting of creditors, the creditors have the opportunity to query the company's affairs and seek to appoint an alternative liquidator if they so choose.

- **The Liquidator**
  The role of the liquidator is discussed further below.

 ## Recent statistics

Below is a graph demonstrating the number of creditors' voluntary liquidations from 2007 to August 2009. As would be expected, the volume of such liquidations has increased dramatically since the last quarter of 2008 and has again increased in volume during the first eight months of 2009.

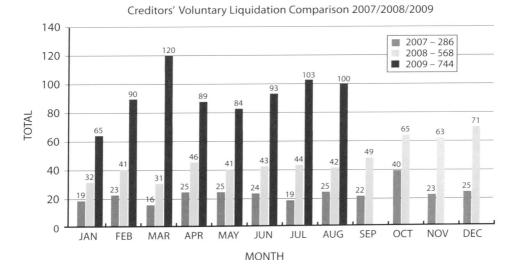

Creditors' Voluntary Liquidation Comparison 2007/2008/2009

Legend:
- 2007 – 286
- 2008 – 568
- 2009 – 744

(Courtesy: www.insolvencyjournal.ie)

 ## The process involved in a creditors' voluntary liquidation

Before deciding whether or not to place their company into liquidation, directors should seek financial advice, either from their auditors, accountants, legal advisors or in certain cases from an insolvency specialist.

Directors who ignore the warning signs of their respective company's insolvency can find themselves trading while insolvent. If it is found that they knew or ought to have known that they were incurring liabilities that the company would not be in a position to pay, the directors, can in certain circumstances, be found personally liable for the debts of the company.

Certain companies may be able to trade out of their difficulties through schemes like examinations or turnaround reconstructions.

However, in this section we deal with companies that have no chance of survival and must be placed into liquidation.

It is a fact that most businesses fail in the first five years of trading, and companies may fail due to a multitude of different reasons. Regardless of the reason behind the collapse of a company, the process for calling a meeting of creditors remains the same.

 ## Planning the meetings of members and creditors

After a first meeting of directors in which the company's financial position is reviewed in detail and the decision is made by its directors to place the company into liquidation, the company must then call a meeting of its members (shareholders) and its creditors.

- Such creditor meetings are called pursuant to section 266 of the Companies Act 1963 (CA 1963) for the purposes set out in sections 267 and 268 of the Act.

- Prior to the issuing of notices by the company to its creditors the company should ensure that their listing of creditors is up-to-date to ensure that all creditors of the company (any and all parties owed money by the company) are notified of the meeting.

- The company must also select a venue for the meeting of creditors. This would usually take place at a venue other than the company's premises but within the area of the company's registered office.

- The company should consider utilising the services of a specialist insolvency solicitor to advise them during the period prior to the holding of the creditors' meeting.

- The company must also work with their financial advisors to prepare the company's Statement of Affairs, which will outline the financial position of the company at the date of the meeting. (The preparation of this document will be dealt with in more detail later in this chapter.)

Notice of the creditors' meeting

There are statutory requirements regarding the notification to creditors, and advertisement of the meeting of creditors, to ensure that the company's creditors are made aware, in good time, of the proposed meeting and given the opportunity to attend.

- The company firstly must place an advertisement of the meeting in two national newspapers 10 days prior to the meeting taking place **(see Appendix 2.1)**. (Best practice is to exclude the day of the meeting of creditors and the day of the advertisement from the 10 days' notice.)

- Send a written notice to the members (shareholders) convening an Extraordinary General Meeting of the company, together with General and Special Proxy Forms, which are essentially voting papers for this meeting **(see Appendix 2.2)**.

- Send a notice of the meeting to the company's creditors, together with General and Special Proxy forms, again giving 10 days' notice of the meeting **(see Appendix 2.3)**.

- Any limited company or partnership who wish to attend the proposed meeting, and have a vote at same, should return their proxy to the company no later than 4 pm on the day prior to the meeting. The return address for proxies is usually specified in the notice and advertisement.

- Individuals do not need to return a proxy if they intend to attend the meeting.

Second Meeting of Directors

Once the statutory notices have been issued, advertisements placed and statement of affairs prepared, a second meeting of the directors of the company must be held in accordance with the company's Articles of Association for the following reasons:

- To appoint one of the directors as chairperson at the respective meetings of creditors and members

- To approve the statement of affairs of the company

- To approve a statement to be read to the company's members and creditors

- To arrange for a sufficient number of copies of the statement of affairs to be available for presentation to the creditors.

This meeting is usually held the day before the meetings of members and creditors.

Directors' Estimated Statement of Affairs

The Directors' Estimated Statement of Affairs is a document prepared by the directors of the company in which it lists:

- The company's assets (under general headings)

- The estimated value of these assets

- Its specific liabilities (individual creditors).

It is the directors' **best estimate** as to the financial position of the company and

includes the assets and liabilities as at the latest practical date before the meeting of creditors.

Directors should note that the liquidator is obliged to send the directors' statement of affairs to the Office of the Director of Corporate Enforcement (ODCE) as part of his or her statutory duties. Though this is an estimated document and is, therefore, not audited, it should be as accurate as possible. There is no prescribed format for the document, though over time and in practice, a relatively standard format has evolved (**see Appendix 2.4**).

Creditors should be listed according to class. The **priority for distribution of assets in a liquidation** is as follows:

- **fixed charge/mortgage holders**
  Usually the company's bankers who have taken security over an asset

- **super preferential claim**
  This is a claim of the Revenue Commissioners in respect of unpaid employee PRSI

- **preferential creditors**
  - *unpaid taxes* (usually) arising in the last 12 months
  - *employee claims* (including those of directors) subject to certain limits
  - *rates* (usually) arising in the last 12 months

- **floating charge**
  Usually the company's bankers who have taken security over an asset of a variable nature, e.g. debtors or stocks

- **unsecured creditors**

The meeting of members (shareholders)

Prior to holding the meeting of creditors, an extraordinary general meeting of the members of the company must take place. This usually takes place immediately before the meeting of creditors. After a review of the company's financial position has been completed (as presented by the directors' estimated statement of affairs), the members resolve that:

- the company is insolvent

- the company is placed in liquidation

- a liquidator is appointed for the purposes of the liquidation.

The liquidator will be appointed by passing an Ordinary Resolution of shareholders, by way of simple majority of members. (**See Appendix 2.5.**)

The meeting of creditors

The meeting of creditors will be opened by the chairman, or a legal representative, who will inform those in attendance of the purpose of the meeting and the relevant legislation under which the meeting has been convened. The following will then occur:

- The meeting will be made aware of the resolutions passed at the earlier meeting of members.

- The chairman of the meeting will then address those in attendance with a statement outlining (predominantly) the history of the company, those involved with the company and how the company came to be in its present position (Statement of Insolvency Practice **S8B: Planning and Administration of Creditors' Meetings** as issued by Chartered Accountants Ireland).

- The chairman or their advisor will then invite questions from those in attendance and request that those asking questions identify themselves and who they represent. (The chairman should address the queries of those in attendance to the best of his ability.)

- Following the conclusion of the queries, the resolution that was passed at the meeting of members will be read once more to those in attendance and the nominated liquidator, again, identified.

- Nominations for an alternative liquidator to be appointed are then requested from those in attendance.

No alternate nominees

If there are no alternate nominees as liquidator, the resolution passed by the company is deemed approved and the members' nominated liquidator is duly appointed.

Alternative nominees

In the event that there is an alternative nominee put forward by the creditors, the following will apply:

- Those in attendance must vote in respect of the nomination. The nominee with the majority vote of creditors (in terms of value – number is no longer relevant) is appointed. The vote will be based on the value of each creditors' outstanding balance as per the company's records or as accepted by the chairperson of the meeting.

- This vote can initially be an informal show of hands or, if necessary, a formal vote by way of written ballot. The vote will be conducted by the chairman of the meeting.

- Votes may be in the favour of the chairman (and therefore the members' nominee) or in favour of the alternate nominee.

- Votes by proxy must be reviewed to ensure they are in order (completed correctly).

- Not every creditor in attendance is obliged to cast a vote and may abstain.

The Committee of Inspection

A committee of inspection is a representative body of members and creditors. Regardless as to whether a vote has occurred following the election of a liquidator under section 268 CA 1963 the creditors will be invited to have a committee of inspection established during the liquidation.

Normally, there are no more than **five** committee members in total and the functions of the committee are:

- liaise with the company's creditors on behalf of the liquidator

- provide the liquidator with information on the company's activities

- aid the liquidator in the investigation of the company's affairs

- approve fees

- approve legal actions

- approve the compromise of debtors

- attend meetings to review the course of the liquidation.

Following the conclusion of the meeting

Following the passing of the resolution to appoint a liquidator to the company and the subsequent confirmation, the liquidator should make himself known to those in attendance.

The liquidator may, if he deems it necessary, call the first meeting of the committee of inspection immediately following the creditors' meeting.

The liquidator's role and function

After the liquidator is appointed at a meeting of creditors, the liquidator becomes an agent of the company and takes over the management of the company in order to realise and distribute the company's assets in accordance with the Companies Acts and to investigate and report on the demise of the company.

As mentioned previously, the Statements of Insolvency Practice are a series of papers setting out basic principles and essential procedures with which every insolvency practitioner is required to comply.

Whether there are assets or not, the liquidator should carry out a sufficient standard of procedure in fulfilling this duty to investigate the company's affairs, and creditors should be confident that the duty to investigate the affairs of the company has been properly discharged.

The **duties and powers that facilitate the liquidator's functions** are outlined below. The liquidator *must*:

1. Take possession of all the Company's assets, including books of account and other documents relevant to its affairs

- A liquidator may apply to the High Court for an order freezing the company's assets, where he or she suspects that they are in danger of dissipation or removal from the jurisdiction by any person.

2. Collate a list of people who are owed money and how much they are owed

- On appointment, the liquidator will write to all known creditors and shareholders of the company requesting that they furnish the liquidator with a statement of account and supporting paperwork for their claim against the company in liquidation.

- On the confirmation of available funds for distribution to the various classes of creditors, the liquidator will review and admit the claims that are bona fide.

- In accordance with section 227(1) CA 1963, the liquidator will also publish a notice in *Iris Oifigiúil* confirming his appointment and deliver to the Registrar of Companies a true original of the Form 16A (G2) confirming his appointment. This provides unknown creditors the opportunity to identify the appointed liquidator and lodge a claim in the liquidation. There is no legal obligation on a liquidator in a creditors' voluntary liquidation to advertise the appointment in a newspaper.

3. Liaise with employees to finalise any claim they may have against the company

- The liquidator will endeavour to assist the employees in preparing their claim to lodge with the Department of Enterprise, Trade and Employment (DETE).

- The liquidator will also ensure that any part of an employee's claim that is not discharged by the DETE will rank accordingly in the liquidation.

4. List the company's assets at date of appointment

- The directors' estimated statement of affairs gives the liquidator an indication of the company's assets.

- A review of the company books and records will confirm the make-up of the company assets, identifying the debtors, fixed assets and other interests.

Once the details have been confirmed, the liquidator will safeguard and seek to collect in all monies due to the company and dispose of any assets or interests that will generate funds for the liquidation.

5. Verify the validity of charges

- SIP S2B requires liquidators to obtain details of all securities held by banks and other parties and the liquidator should check the registration and confirm the validity of the charge.

- A liquidator may render a charge void under section 288 CA 1963 if it was registered within 12 months of the liquidation and the company was not solvent immediately after its creation.

- A floating charge created within two years of an insolvent liquidation may be invalid if the charge was in favour of a director or a person connected to a director.

6. Verify the validity of prior insolvency appointments

- Where a company is placed in liquidation after a receivership, the validity of the receiver's appointment should be confirmed in accordance with SIP S2B (Liquidator's Investigation).

- Where liquidation follows examination, to the extent that significant matters have not been brought to the court's attention during the examination process, the conduct of the company's affairs during the examination should be reviewed.

7. Disclaim unprofitable contracts

- The liquidator may disclaim unprofitable contracts under section 290 CA 1963 within 12 months of the winding up or such extended period as is allowed by the court.

- The liquidator may abandon a contract or property which is no longer profitable.

- The court may require notice of disclaimer to be given to any person interested, and impose such conditions as it thinks just. This act does not affect the rights of any other persons.

8. Pay the company debts in the following order:

- The fixed charges in the order in which they were created (in so far as not previously realised outside the liquidation e.g. through a receivership).

- The costs of the liquidation, including the liquidator's remuneration.

- The preferential debts in order of:

  - super preferential debts

  - preferential debts (those listed below have equal standing):
    - *The Revenue Commissioners*
    - *former employees*
    - *commercial rates*

  - the floating charges, in the order in which they were created

  - the unsecured creditors

  - distribute any remaining money to the shareholders in line with their entitlements

The consent of the committee of inspection is required where the liquidator wishes to pay any class of creditors in full, or make a compromise or arrangement with creditors.

9. Investigate the company's affairs

(The liquidators' investigations and reporting of same are reviewed briefly later in this chapter, and examined in greater detail in **Chapter 7.**)

10. Report any suspected criminal offence by the company, a past or present director, secretary or any member to the ODCE and the Director of Public Prosecutions (DPP).

11. Apply to the High Court to **restrict each of the directors from being involved** in other companies unless the obligation is removed by the ODCE.

12. Write a report on the winding up

13. Convene a meeting of members and a meeting of creditors at the end of the first year of the winding up process and at the end of each subsequent year.

14. Deliver a final statement of the receipt and payments to the Companies' Registration Office

- In a voluntary liquidation, the company will be dissolved three months after the final papers have been lodged with the Companies Registration Office (CRO).

The liquidator has powers:

- to dispose of the company assets

  In the event that the liquidator wishes to sell, subject to certain limits, non-cash items to any individual who was an officer of the company within three years before winding up, the liquidator will issue 14 days' notice to the creditors confirming his intention to do so.

- to initiate or defend any legal or other action in the name of or on behalf of the company

- to carry on trading for as long as is deemed necessary by the liquidator

- to execute all deeds in the name of the company

- to take out loans and give corporate assets as security

- to do whatever is necessary for the successful winding-up and distribution of the assets among creditors.

In summary, the liquidator may employ any or all of the above powers and duties to fulfil his/her function of realising and distributing the company assets and investigating and reporting on the demise of the company.

 ## Investigations

The purpose of an investigation is to identify the assets and liabilities of the company, to determine the reasons for the failure of the company, and to review the conduct, decisions and actions of the directors. This investigation forms the basis of the liquidator's report to the Office of the Director of Corporate Enforcement (ODCE).

The liquidators of insolvent companies have a statutory obligation to report to the ODCE pursuant to section 56 of the Company Law Enforcement Act 2001 (CLEA 2001) within six months of the date of their appointment. Section 56 CLEA 2001 amends section 150 CA 1990 by introducing an obligation on liquidators of insolvent companies to bring a restriction application against the directors of the company, unless relieved from this obligation by the Director of Corporate Enforcement. For the sake of clarity, this obligation remains even in circumstances where the company in liquidation has no assets to pay for same.

On receipt of the first report, the ODCE decides to what extent the liquidator should be definitively relieved from the statutory obligation to take High Court

restriction proceedings against the company's directors.

Where liquidators are granted additional time to complete investigations by the issue of 'relief at this time' letters, the requirement for further reports will continue until such time as the Director of Corporate Enforcement is in a position to make a final decision. At that stage, the automatic requirement for further reports will cease.

The ODCE will continue to require liquidators to inform them of the progress and eventual outcome of restriction applications where they arise.

The ODCE reserve the right, in all cases, to request further reports at any time where they consider that the circumstances of a particular case deem it to be appropriate.

In addition, the ODCE may, from time to time, seek reports on the progress of individual liquidations and seek explanations for any undue delays in completing them.

Section 56 CLEA 2001 places an obligation on liquidators to investigate the affairs of an insolvent company and to comment on particular areas of the Directors' conduct. These areas, plus possible litigation that can arise from such investigations, are further explored in **Chapter 7**.

Closing a creditors' voluntary liquidation

- Ensure all assets have been realised

- Finalise any pension, insurance or assurance matters

- Finalise payments to preferential and unsecured creditors

- If a deposit account was opened in the case, complete the relevant corporation tax returns for any deposit interest that is payable

- Close all bank accounts

- Ensure all pre-liquidation tax returns are submitted where possible. If not possible, inform the Revenue Commissioners of the reasons.

- Ensure all post-liquidation taxes are returned and paid

- Inform the liquidator's legal advisor of the final meeting and seek assurance that there are no outstanding matters

- Obtain written clearance from the Collector General and relevant Inspector of Taxes, both pre- and post-liquidation

- De-register for VAT and any other taxes

- Notify all members of the final meeting

- Notify all creditors of the final meeting

- Notify the ODCE of the final meeting

- Notify the Collector General of the final meeting

- Call final meeting of Committee of Inspection

- Inform the Department of Enterprise, Trade and Employment of the Final Meeting and status of any preferential dividend

- Place a notice of the final members' and creditors' meetings in **two** national daily newspapers at least 28 days in advance of the meeting

- Send a cover letter to creditors (re-)informing them of the final meeting and the dividend outcome in this case. It would be considered best practice to issue the final notice at the same time as the advertisement is placed

- Send a cover letter to members informing of the final meeting and case outcome with similar timing to the advertisement

- Submit signed Form 13A/F14 CRO forms within seven days after the Final Meeting

- Forward copy **Form 14** to:
  - Revenue Commissioners
  - The DETE
  - ODCE

Case Study – *Tralee Beef and Lamb Limited (2008)*

Background to the Supreme Court Judgment

T om Kavanagh was appointed liquidator of Tralee Beef and Lamb Limited ("the company") in January 2002. At the date of his appointment, the company had four directors.

The company was in the business of slaughtering cattle and lambs, and had been quite clearly affected by the BSE outbreaks and associated developments prior to its liquidation.

Under section 56 of the CLEA 2001, the liquidator was obliged to submit a detailed report on the stewardship of the directors. The liquidator formed a view that one of the directors, a non-executive director, had acted honestly and responsibly in relation to the affairs of the company.

The liquidator requested from the Director of Corporate Enforcement (ODCE) to be relieved from the statutory obligation to bring restriction proceedings in relation to this director, but the ODCE declined this request. At the time, the ODCE was not obliged to give, nor was it in the practice of giving, a reason for declining a request for relief.

Tom Kavanagh brought the restriction proceedings pursuant to section 150 CA 1990, as was his obligation, and on 20 July 2004, all of the company's directors were restricted by order of the High Court.

The restriction order made against the non-executive director became the subject of considerable publicity and an appeal to the Supreme Court.

Given that the liquidator had found the non-executive director to have acted honestly and responsibly in the first instance, he was never likely to object to the appeal. Furthermore, under the relevant legislation, a liquidator is not obliged to defend an appeal, and similarly ODCE are not obligated to become involved. The liquidator invited the ODCE to takeover the proceedings. However, while the ODCE prepared to offer legal submissions, they refused to join the proceedings.

According to the Supreme Court judgment, the ODCE gave no reasons for their decision to refuse relief.

The Supreme Court said that the statutory regime relating to the restriction of directors could be regarded as a draconian one for a number of reasons. These reasons included: first, the mandatory obligation on a liquidator to bring an application; secondly that a restriction order must be made unless the director satisfies the Court that he acted honestly and responsibly, which is a reversal of the normal burden of proof; and finally, the Court observed that, where the respondent is a professional man, in this instance a chartered accountant, the effect of a restriction order would be much greater than if he was a "cowboy" director because of the reputational damage that would be caused.

The Court **held** that the non-executive director had a legitimate ground of complaint on three grounds, which may be summarised as the "amplification" of the duties of a director, the specific position of the director within the company and conflict with a fellow director.

Amplification of duties

A feature of the original High Court decision was that the Supreme Court found it had amplified the duties which a director should comply with, including what the High Court judge called "duties of loyalty based on fiduciary principles, developed initially by the Courts of Equity and duties of skill and care developed initially by the Common Law Courts from the principles in the law of negligence". While the Supreme Court did not disagree with the content of the High Court's amplification, it felt that in a hearing of great importance to the director, where his reputation and professional standing were intricately involved, it was not appropriate to amplify the director's duties or otherwise the criteria for imposing on him what is a very significant stigma, particularly where the director had been expressly found to have been honest in his dealings.

According to the Supreme Court judgment, the amplification was made by the High Court Judge "after the hearing" which did not give the director an opportunity to present "detailed argument as to the content and wording of the amplification" in circumstances where the effect of the High Court's amplification would have a considerable significance for his reputation. This was a key factor underpinning the Supreme Court's decision to allow the director's appeal.

The position of the director

The Supreme Court effectively suggested that in looking to previous High Court cases for guidance that the size of the companies involved needs to be taken into account. The Court said that duties imposed on a highly paid executive director of a vast bank may be of limited use in considering the common law duties of a non-executive director appointed to keep BES investors informed in relation to the workings of a small company. The Court said that care must be taken to avoid being unrealistic in relation to a small meat company in rural Ireland ran effectively by a sole executive director.

Conflict with fellow director

The High Court Judge remarked that there was considerable conflict in affidavits between the non-executive appellant director and the managing director of the company. It appeared to the Supreme Court that the managing director's evidence was in effect treated as part of the case against his fellow director. The Supreme Court felt that given that the liquidator himself did not believe that the non-executive director should be restricted, that it was somewhat unsatisfactory that the evidence against the director was that of a person resisting his own restriction, i.e. defending his own conduct of affairs as a director by trying in so far as he could to shift the blame on to a fellow director.

The Court said that it may not be proper to consider what other directors said in their own defence as a part of the case against the director, on the basis that such an approach deprived the director of part at least of the benefit of the fact that the liquidator had concluded he had acted honestly and responsibly.

Ramifications of Case

The outcome of the case featured prominently in the 2008 Annual Report of the Director of Corporate Enforcement and, as a direct result of the case, the Director of Corporate Enforcement now outlines the reasons why it does not grant relief in circumstances where the decision of the liquidator was to seek relief from the obligation to bring restriction proceedings pursuant to section 150 of the Companies Act 1990. The obligation on the liquidator to bring restriction proceedings still, however, remains.

The case again placed the spotlight on the role and responsibility of non-executive directors and, despite the successful appeal, a reluctance amongst venture capitalists to take on the mantle of a directorship of a company receiving investment has been evident.

Finally, the Supreme Court comments unfavourably on the reversal of the burden of proof under which section 150 CA 1990 operates. Could this be possible grounds for a challenge to a restriction decision on constitutional grounds?

 Frequently Asked Questions

Q) Who is responsible for conducting the meeting of creditors?

A) A director of the company is responsible for chairing the meeting and may be advised by a third party.

Q) What information must be provided to those in attendance?

A) Each creditor must be given a Statement of Affairs outlining the financial position of the company.

Q) Can the company's accountant/auditor chair the meeting of creditors?

A) No. A director of the company must chair the meeting of creditors.

Q) My client is a director of a company going into liquidation, is he allowed to buy back the assets?

A) A director is allowed to buy back assets but the liquidator is obliged to inform all known creditors of the proposed sale and give 14 days notice before completing any such sale.

Q) Should the company's accountant/auditor attend the meeting of creditors?

A) If a creditor, the company's accountant/auditor is entitled to attend the meeting. However, it would not generally be recommended as creditors can often seek to have the accountant/auditor answer questions about the company's affairs which should be properly directed to the chairperson/director.

Q) Can the company's accountant/ auditor act as the liquidator?

A) No. This would be a conflict of interest.

Q) What is the purpose of the creditors' meeting?

A) The meeting of creditors is a meeting which must be held under company Law to ratify the appointment of a liquidator to a company.

Q) If a creditor does not attend the meeting can they still submit a claim against the company?

A) A creditor is not obliged to attend the meeting of creditors and will still have a valid claim against the company in the liquidation.

Q) Can a creditor allow a third party attend in their place at the meeting?

A) Yes. A creditor can nominate a representative to be their proxy at the meeting.

Q) Who pays for the advertisements and hotel room for the meeting of creditors?

A) If funds are available, the company can pay these costs as a necessary cost for the winding up. Similarly, the costs of a solicitor for the meeting of creditors and accountant's fees for preparation of the statement of affairs can be discharged as a cost for the winding up of the company. If funds are not available, then the directors must personally pay these costs as once the company enters liquidation such costs are unsecured and cannot be paid by the liquidator.

Q) Once a liquidator is appointed can directors wash their hands of the company?

A) Absolutely not. Although the directors' powers cease on the appointment of a liquidator, their responsibilities and duties remain. Of particular note is that a failure to co-operate with a liquidator has been successfully used as a reason for the restriction of directors.

Q) How long does a liquidation take?

A) Statutory requirements mean that it is unlikely that even a relatively small and straightforward liquidation will be completed within a year.

Q) Do I invite employees to the meeting of creditors?

A) If the employees have unpaid claims against the company be it for redundancy, minimum notice, wages, holiday pay, expenses etc., they are considered to be a creditor of the company and should be notified of the meeting of creditors.

Q) My company is based in Terenure, Dublin 6. Can I hold the meeting of creditors in Donegal?

A) No. The meeting of creditors must be held in the area of the registered office of the company. If the location of the meeting is challenged in Court, a Judge may allow a certain amount of leeway if it can be proven that holding the meeting in the location decided upon facilitated attendance by creditors.

Q) What are the financial costs of restriction?

A) The costs can vary considerably depending on the extent to which the application is defended and the level of investigation carried out to respond to affidavits. The High Court has, however, indicated a costs order of €1,500 including VAT for an undefended restriction. The directors would, however, have to pay their own representation costs also.

Q) If a director successfully defends a restriction application, can he get his costs back from the liquidator?

A) The matter of costs is under the jurisdiction of the presiding Judge. However, the High Court would not usually make an order against the liquidator for costs as the onus is on the director to prove that he has acted honestly and responsibly.

In the event that a liquidator has erred in his decision to bring the proceedings or failed in his investigation of the affairs of the company, the High Court may make a costs order against the liquidator.

Q) If a company goes into liquidation, are the directors immediately restricted from acting as a director of another company?

A) No. The directors only become restricted if the Office of the Director of Corporate Enforcement requires the liquidator to bring proceedings and on the hearing of the proceedings, the High Court makes an order of restriction. In reality, this will take a minimum of a year after the liquidation commences.

Q) Does a liquidator have to give directors a copy of the Section 56 report?

A) A liquidator is obliged to disclose only certain parts of the report to directors once a restriction application has been issued. It should be noted, however, that the liquidator will invariably raise matters of

concern with the directors prior to the submission of the Section 56 report. Indeed, the High Court has been critical of liquidators who have failed to give directors the opportunity to explain their actions prior to the submission of the Section 56 report.

Q) Who prepares the Statement of Affairs?

A) Under the Companies Act 1963, the directors of the company are obliged to present a Statement of Affairs. The statement of affairs generally shows the book value of the company's assets together with their realisable value. The statement of affairs should also have a list of the company's creditors and the amount of each claim.

Q) Who is considered as a director for the purpose of the liquidator's investigation?

A) When the liquidator files his/her report with the Office of Director of Corporate Enforcement, the liquidator will consider all individuals who are recorded with the Companies Registration Office within the 12 months prior to the creditors meeting. The liquidator will also include any individual or company that he / she believes was acting as a de facto director or shadow director.

Q) What should I include in the Chairman's statement?

A) The directors should give an outline of the history of the company and reasons for its failure. This should be as comprehensive as possible and deal with any contentious issues.

Q) Can the creditors nominate an alternative liquidator to the members' nominee liquidator?

A) To reject the members' nominee and replace him/her with a creditors nominee will require that the majority in value of the creditors validly voting at the creditors' meeting vote in favour of their nominee.

Q) Should the directors sell the assets of the company if the company is insolvent?

A) In general, directors should not dispose of the assets of an insolvent company and a liquidator should be appointed to complete the sale of same. There is, however, an obligation on the directors to safeguard all the assets of the company until such time as the liquidator is appointed to the company. This may, in certain circumstances, warrant the sale of assets by the directors at a time when the company is insolvent. An obvious example of this would be when the assets may lose value if not disposed of immediately.

Q) Can a director's personal guarantee be enforced before the end of the liquidation?

A) The status of the liquidation would not usually have any bearing of note on personal guarantees. Where it is clear that there is likely to be a substantial shortfall in the available realisations as opposed to the outstanding debt, a guarantor will almost certainly pursue the personal guarantee regardless of the progress of the liquidation.

Q) The liquidation has been completed, can the company's records be destroyed?

A) The company's records cannot be destroyed for a period of three years after the final meeting. It is important to bear this in mind when collecting records at the commencement of the liquidation especially if the records are also available in digital format. The liquidator's own files must be retained for a period of six years after the completion of the liquidation.

Q) My client's company is insolvent but he is going to let it be struck off rather than liquidate. Is this a viable option?

A) The Director of Corporate Enforcement is targeting cases such as these and has already had disqualification orders made against many such directors. The exposure to a disqualification order is further amplified by potential criminal sanctions that the Director of Corporate Enforcement may seek. In short, this is a not a practice to be recommended.

– Appendix 2.1 –

Sample Newspaper Advertisement of Creditors' Meeting

In the Matter of
COMPANIES ACTS, 1963 TO 2009
and
In the Matter of

<u>Unknown Limited</u>

NOTICE IS HEREBY GIVEN pursuant to Section 266(2) of the Companies Act, 1963, that a Meeting of the Creditors of the above named company will be held at The Hotel, Ballsbridge Road, Ballsbridge, Dublin 4 on the 26th day of July 2009 at 10.15 a.m. for the purposes mentioned in Sections 267 and 268 of the said Act.

Dated this 10th day of July 2009
By Order of the Board

Note:
Proxies to be used at the meeting must be lodged with the company at Unit 25c, The Business Park, Nangor Road, Dublin 22 not later than 4.00 p.m. on the 25th day of July 2009.

– Appendix 2.2 –

Members' Notice
General and Special Proxy Forms

In the Matter of
COMPANIES ACTS, 1963 TO 2009
and
In the Matter of

<u>Unknown Limited</u>

NOTICE IS HEREBY GIVEN that an extraordinary general meeting of the company will be held at The Hotel, Ballsbridge Road, Ballsbridge, Dublin 4 on the 26th day of July 2009 at 10am for the purpose of considering and, if thought fit, passing the following Resolutions:

1] "It has been proved to the satisfaction of this Meeting that the Company cannot, by reason of its liabilities, continue its business and that it is advisable to wind up same and that accordingly, the Company be, and is hereby wound up voluntarily".

2] "Mr. Tom Kavanagh of Kavanagh Fennell of Simmonscourt Road, Dublin 4, be appointed Liquidator."

Dated this 10th day of July 2009
By Order of the Board

Notes:
A member entitled to attend and vote is entitled to appoint a proxy to attend, speak and vote instead of him and a proxy need not be a member (a form of proxy is enclosed herewith). Proxies to be used at the meeting must be lodged with the company at Unit 25c, The Business Park, Nangor Road, Dublin 22 not later than 4.00 p.m. on the 25th day of July 2009.

GENERAL PROXY

In the Matter of
COMPANIES ACTS, 1963 TO 2009
and
In the Matter of

Unknown Limited

I/We .... of ....

in the County of .... being a Member/Members of the above

mentioned company hereby appoint

(1) (a) .... of ....

or failing him (b) .... of ....

as my/our proxy to vote at the Meeting of Members to be held on the 26th day of July 2009 or at any adjournment thereof to vote for/against the Resolution in the Notice of the Meeting.

Dated this   day of   2009

(Signed) (Note 2) _____

Notes:

1]   The person appointed proxy may be the Chairman of the Meeting, or any such person as the Member may appoint. The Proxy Form should be altered accordingly.

2]   If a Firm, then sign the Firm's trading name and add "by A.B. a Partner in the said Firm". If the appointed is a Corporation, the form of Proxy must be under its common seal or under the hand of some Officer duly authorised in that behalf and the fact that the officer is so authorised must also be stated.

3]   This Proxy, when signed, must be lodged by the time and at the address named for that purpose in the Notice convening the Meeting at which it is to be used.

SPECIAL PROXY

In the Matter of

COMPANIES ACTS, 1963 TO 2009

and

In the Matter of

Unknown Limited

I/We ....

of ....

a Member of the above mentioned company hereby appoint

(1) ....

or (failing him)

....of ....

to be my/our proxy at the meeting of members to be held on the 26th day of July 2009 or any adjournment thereof.

(a) ....

Dated this   day of   2009

(Signed) (Note2) _____

Notes:

1] The person appointed proxy may be the Chairman of the Meeting, or any such person as the Member may appoint. The Proxy Form should be altered accordingly.

2] Here insert the word "for" or the word "against" as the case may require and complete as desired.

3] If a Firm, then sign the Firm's trading name and add "by A.B. a Partner in the said Firm". If the appointed is a Corporation, the form of Proxy must be under its common seal or under the hand of some Officer duly authorised in that behalf and the fact that the officer is so authorised must also be stated.

4] This Proxy, when signed, must be lodged by the time and at the address named for that purpose in the Notice convening the Meeting at which it is to be used.

– Appendix 2.3 –

Creditors' Notice
General and Special Proxy Forms

In the Matter of

COMPANIES ACTS, 1963 TO 2009

and

In the Matter of

<u>Unknown Limited</u>

NOTICE IS HEREBY GIVEN pursuant to Section 266(1) of the Companies Act, 1963, that a Meeting of the Creditors of the above named company will be held at The Hotel, Ballsbridge Road, Ballsbridge, Dublin 4 on the 26th day of July 2009 at 10.15 a.m. for the purposes mentioned in Sections 267 and 268 of the said Act.

Dated this 10th day of July 2009
By Order of the Board

Note:
Proxies to be used at the meeting must be lodged with the company at Unit 25c, The Business Park, Nangor Road, Dublin 22 not later than 4.00 p.m. on the 25th day of July 2009.

GENERAL PROXY

In the Matter of

COMPANIES ACTS, 1963 TO 2009

and

In the Matter of

Unknown Limited

I/We .... of ....

a Creditor of the above mentioned company, hereby appoint

(1)..

or, failing him

(2)..

to be my/our General Proxy to vote at the Meeting of Creditors to be held in the above matter on the 26th day of July 2009 or at any adjournment thereof.

Dated this　　　　day of　　　　2009

(Signed) (Note 2) _____

Notes:

1]　The person appointed General Proxy may be the Chairman of the Meeting or such other person as the Creditor may appoint. The Proxy Form should be completed accordingly.

2]　If a Firm, sign the Firm's trading name and add "by A.B. a partner in the said Firm". Where this Form of Proxy is executed by a Corporation, it must be either under its common seal or under the hand of an Officer or Attorney duly authorised in that behalf, and the fact that the officer is so authorised must also be stated.

3]　This Proxy, when signed, must be lodged by the time and at the address named for that purpose in the Notice convening the Meeting at which it is to be used.

SPECIAL PROXY

In the Matter of
COMPANIES ACTS, 1963 TO 2009
and
In the Matter of

<u>Unknown Limited</u>

I/We ....

of ....

a Creditor, hereby appoint

(1) ....

of ....

or (failing him)

....of ....

to be my/our Special Proxy at the Meeting of Creditors to be held in the above matter on 26th day of July 2009, or at any adjournment thereof, and to vote (2)　　　　　　the Resolution in the Notice convening the said meeting.

Dated this　　　　　day of　　　　　2009

(Signed) (Note2) _____

Notes:

1] The person appointed Special Proxy may be the Chairman of the Meeting, or any such person as the Creditor may appoint. The Proxy Form should be altered accordingly. A Creditor may give a Special Proxy to any person to vote at any specified meeting or adjournment thereof on all or any matters arising at the meeting.

2] Here insert the word "for" or the word "against" as the case may require and complete as desired.

3] If a Firm, then sign the Firm's trading name and add "by A.B. a Partner in the said Firm". If the appointed is a Corporation, the form of Proxy must be under its common seal or under the hand of some Officer duly authorised in that behalf and the fact that the officer is so authorised must also be stated.

4] This Proxy, when signed, must be lodged by the time and at the address named for that purpose in the Notice convening the Meeting at which it is to be used.

– Appendix 2.4 –
Directors' Estimated Statement of Affairs

Unknown Limited

Directors' Estimated Statement of Affairs as at 26th July 2009

	Net Book Value €	Estimated To Realise €	Estimated To Realise €
Leased Assets			
Computer Equipment	12,257	6,129	
Office Equipment	11,389	5,000	11,129
Less Leasing Liabilities			-18,173
			0
Secured Assets			
Debtors	350,000	275,000	
Less Secured Financing thereon		-250,000	25,000
Fixed Assets			
Leasehold Premises	271,724	0	
Computer Equipment	3,415	2,000	
Office Equipment	25,490	5,000	
Service Equipment	34,153	25,000	32,000
Other Assets			
Cash at bank	3,910	3,910	
Stocks	60,750	48,600	
Unencumbered Debtors	79,844	55,891	108,401
Funds Available for Distribution to Super Preferential Creditors			165,401
Super Preferential Creditors			-7,400
Funds Available for Distribution to Preferential Creditors			158,001
Preferential Creditors		*Note 1*	-77,395
Funds Available for Distribution to Floating Chargeholder			**88,006**
Floating Chargeholder			-75,000
Funds Available for Distribution to Unsecured Creditors			**13,006**
Unsecured Creditors		*Note 2*	-88,878
Deficiency as regards Unsecured Creditors			**-75,872**

Signed _____

A Director

B Director

Appendix 2.4 – cont.

Unknown Limited

Preferential creditors as at 26th July 2008

Note 1

		€	€
Revenue Commissioners	PAYE	25,000	
	VAT	42,895	67,895
Staff Entitlements:			7,500
Commercial Rates			2,000
Total Preferential Creditors			**77,395**

Appendix 2.4 – cont.

Unknown Limited

Unsecured creditors as at 26th July 2008

Note 2

		€
AGA		26
Adrienne Malone		12,417
A Leasing Company	Shortfall re: leasing	7,045
Al Molloy		8,630
Bank Overdraft		5,744
Bank Floating chargeholder		75,000
Caitlin Gallagher		2,500
Conor Roberts Toulson		2,500
Electricity Provider		450
Emmet Briggs		14,371
Fortune & Son Builder		109
Gas Company		874
Geraldine The Plasterer		233
Graham The Wheeler Dealer		3,054
Insurance Company		813
John Como		4,000
John Perry		4,298
Leinster News		1,419
Local Authority Water Rates		1,855
Local Authority Commercial Rates		2,000
Revenue Commissioners		67,895
Ronald Dough		5,410
Sean Sheils		2,500
Security Company		11,216
South Dublin Co Co		4,124
Petrol Company		150
Phone Company		983
Van Repair Company		171
Waste Removal Company		1,486

Total Creditors	**241,273**
Less Preferential Creditors	-77,395
Less Floating Chargeholders	-75,000
Total Unsecured Creditors	**88,878**

Note 3
No provision has been made for the costs and expenses of the liquidation

– Appendix 2.5 –
Ordinary Resolution

Certificate Number: 111111   Form N° 16A

COMPANIES ACTS, 1963 TO 1999

Ordinary Resolution
of
Unknown
LIMITED

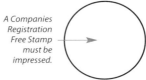

A Companies
Registration
Free Stamp
must be
impressed.

Passed on   26th July 2009

AT A GENERAL MEETING of the Members of the said Company, duly

convened and held at **The Hotel, Ballsbridge Road, Ballsbridge, Dublin 4**

in the   26th   day of   July   20 09

The Ordinary Resolution to be PRINTED on this space and not affixed to it. THE ACT DOES NOT ADMIT OF WRITING.

the following **Ordinary Resolution(s)** was/were duly passed:

1] "It has been proved to the satisfaction of this Meeting that the Company cannot, by reason of its liabilities, continue its business and that it is advisable to wind up same and that accordingly, the Company be, and is hereby wound up voluntarily".

2] "Mr. Tom Kavanagh of Simmonscourt Road, Ballsbridge, Dublin 4 be appointed liquidator for the purposes of the winding up."

Signed   _____

Officer   CHAIRMAN

To be Authenticated by the written Signature of an Officer of the Company.

Signature   _____

Officer   _____

Chapter >> 3

Receiverships

Chapter 3 Overview

What is a receivership?

When a borrower has defaulted on a loan, a receivership is a method by which a mortgage or charge holder (usually a financial institution) will appoint a receiver to attempt to recover the outstanding borrowings.

A receiver has the duty to:

● secure the asset(s) of the company,

● realise the asset(s), and/or

● manage the affairs of the company with a view to maximising the return to the charge holder.

Legislation, and guidance from Chartered Accountants Ireland

The main laws governing the appointment of receivers, their roles and obligations are contained in:

● Part VII (sections 314–323) of the Companies Acts 1963–1990

● Part VI (sections 144–145) and Part VIII (sections 170–179) of the Companies Act 1990 (CA 1990) and sections 52, 53, 55 and 58 of the Company Law Enforcement Act 2001 (CLEA 2001).

Other key legislation governing receiverships includes:

● Conveyancing and Law of Property Act 1881

● Supreme Court of Judicature Act (Ireland) 1877

It should also be noted that the High Court has the power to appoint a receiver by way of equitable execution under the Rules of the Superior Courts where no registered debenture exists:

Example of a court appointed receiver

You have obtained a judgment against a party and you become aware that this party has an entitlement to shares or funds which they do not presently possess. The Court will, in special circumstances make an Order appointing a receiver over such shares, funds or entitlements and they must then in due course be made to the receiver.

Statements of Insolvency Practice are issued by Chartered Accountants Ireland to insolvency practitioners with a view to maintaining standards by setting out required practice and harmonising members' approach to particular aspects of insolvency. The purpose of the Statements of Insolvency Practice is to set out basic principles and essential procedures with which insolvency practitioners are required to comply. A number of Statements of Insolvency Practice govern the position and responsibilities of a receiver:

● S1B: A Receiver's Responsibility for the Company's Records

● S14B: A Receiver's Responsibility to preferential creditors

When is a receivership suitable/appropriate?

A receivership is suitable and/or appropriate:

- where a company is being placed in liquidation by its officers or where the company is under threat of liquidation or the subject of a winding-up order

- when a company is seeking to restructure its finances or make arrangements with its creditors but has not sought the protection of the court by means of seeking the appointment of an examiner

- the principal under a debenture is in arrears

- the interest under a debenture is in arrears

- if a company ceases to trade or carry on business

- if, as a result of some other occurrence the security of the debenture has become threatened

- when the mortgagee has failed to engage the bank to discuss arrears or cash flow problems.

Who are the key parties involved?

While, the process of placing a company into receivership is discussed further below, **the main parties involved in the appointment of a receiver include:**

- the debenture or charge holder (the appointee)

- the debenture or charge holder's legal advisors

- the proposed receiver

- the proposed receiver's legal advisors

- the signatories to the debenture or charge.

Recent statistics

Below is a graph showing the number of receiverships from 2007 to August 2009. As would be expected, the volume of receiverships increased considerably towards the last quarter of 2008 and have dramatically increased in volume during 2009.

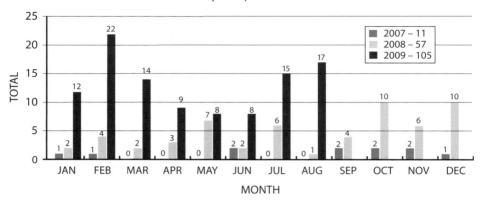

Receivership Comparison 2007/2008/2009

Legend:
- 2007 – 11
- 2008 – 57
- 2009 – 105

(**Note:** 2009 figures are to the end of August 2009)

Commencing the process of receivership

A receiver may be appointed by:

- the High Court pursuant to the Rules of the Superior Court, or

- by means of Equitable Execution (that is, where a judgment has previously been obtained against a debtor that does not possess sufficient assets to discharge the debt and at some point assets or future assets are identified that may not yet have come into the possession of the debtor.

However, the most common method for a receiver to be appointed is under the powers given to a charge holder in a debenture or charge document.

The debenture or charge document will outline the circumstances in which a receiver may be appointed.

As the effect of the appointment of a receiver will, in most (but not all)

circumstances lead to the cessation of and/or sale of the business, it is important that a thorough legal review of the relevant documents takes place prior to the proposed appointment and that the parties are satisfied that the conditions outlined for the appointment of a receiver are met in full.

The solicitor advising the proposed receiver will usually:

- examine the company's memorandum and articles of association to ensure the company possessed the ability to create the debenture and

- check that the debenture was duly sealed in accordance with the company's articles of association.

Further items reviewed at this time include checking to ensure that:

- the debenture was properly created, registered, etc.

- the charge was properly registered within the 21-day time limit

- the debenture could not be deemed as a fraudulent preference having been registered within 12 months of the company entering into liquidation or at a point when the company was insolvent

- property covering the charge is identifiable and the extent of this property.

The appointment of a receiver

A receiver is usually appointed when the debenture or charge holder believes there to be a situation where the terms under which the debenture or charge was granted have been breached and that the most effective way to safeguard the charge holder's position is to appoint a receiver.

The **debenture or charge document**, which is created to coincide with the granting of loan facilities, must contain the specific conditions, which, if occurring, can lead to the appointment of a receiver. In most cases, the document specifies that a written demand must be made for the repayment of the debt in full within a specified time period (usually 24 hours), after which time, if not repaid in full, the guarantor is deemed to be in default. This triggers the power of the debenture or charge holder to appoint a receiver.

The adequacy of this demand may, sometimes, be so clear that a formal demand is not always necessary. However, this is ultimately decided by reference to the terms of the debenture or charge.

A default on a loan repayable on specified dates is very clear. However, for prudence, it is usual that a formal demand is made in most circumstances to ensure compliance

on the part of the appointment process.

The debenture or charge holder must have the necessary power to appoint the receiver – in certain circumstances this may require the approval of the board of the financial institution to pass the relevant resolution authorising the appointment.

At this point, the proposed receiver's legal advisors will usually carry out a complete review of the security documentation surrounding the asset(s), which is/are the subject of the debenture or charge to satisfy themselves that all of the required security is valid.

The debenture or charge holder's legal advisors shall then prepare a **deed of appointment**. The deed sets out the security under which the receiver is appointed and grants the receiver authority to take possession and secure the assets as specified.

The deed of appointment specifies the role of the receiver, which can be either: receiver or receiver and manager; the latter provides the receiver with powers to continue to trade a business should he deem this to be in the best interests of the debenture or charge holder.

This deed of appointment is then witnessed and sealed by the appointing charge holder and signed and witnessed by the receiver. The document also contains the date and time of appointment.

Following the receipt by the proposed receiver of the deed of appointment, or express notice of its existence is received, the receiver is deemed to be in place.

Checklist prior to appointment

Prior to the appointment the following should take place:

- a full review of all security documentation

- a full review of the debenture/charge document and to confirm that the power to appoint a receiver exists

- adequate notice of demand has been sent to the company in the prescribed format and method

- the designated receiver does not fall within those persons or bodies as outlined under sections 314 and 315 of the Companies Act 1963 (CA 1963), which identifies those persons that cannot act as a receiver.

Different types of charges and appointments

The appointment of a receiver is dependent upon the debenture or charge document. A receiver may be appointed over:

- Assets subject to a fixed and floating charge

  - The most common form of appointment is where assets/ security are subject to a fixed and floating charge. Generally, the receiver takes control of all of the company assets and is then in a position to decide on the best course of action to undertake.

- Assets subject to a fixed charge.

  - In this situation, the receiver takes possession of, or responsibility for, specific assets such as a property, machinery, etc. This usually results in the demise of the company.

- Assets subject to a floating charge

  - Where the receiver is appointed over assets subject to a floating charge, it is usual for the receiver to take steps to identify and discharge all of the preferential creditors who take preference over the floating charge holder prior to discharging the amounts owed to the floating charge holder. The list of preferential creditors is set out in section 285 CA1963.

- Assets where no charge is in place (equitable execution)

  - In this situation, where a judgment against a corporate body has been obtained and where assets have been identified that have not yet come into the possession of the corporate body, the High Court appoints a receiver over this future entitlement, and the receiver seeks to take possession of or realise this future asset.

Fixed versus Floating Charges – Specifics

A receiver must be conscious of the type of charge(s) under which they are appointed. This is particularly relevant when considering the rules of priority as set out under section 98 CA 1963.

Receiver is appointed under a fixed charge

Where a receiver is appointed under a fixed charge he is entitled to pass the proceeds of the sale of the fixed charge asset(s) to the debenture holder in full following the payment of the costs and expenses of the receivership.

One anomaly that exists here is on the sale of property assets. The receiver must ensure that any taxation liabilities that may arise as a result of the sale are discharged, e.g. capital gains taxes.

On property assets, it is very important to review the VAT history of the asset being sold, and specialist tax advice may be required.

One further consideration is the discharge of commercial rates outstanding on the property. It is usual that the purchaser's solicitors shall seek confirmation that the asset is free from encumbrances, and since property rates stay with the property until discharged in full these are almost always required to be discharged.

Receiver is appointed under a fixed and floating charge

Where a receiver is appointed under a fixed and floating charge, he is entitled to pass the proceeds of the sale of the fixed asset(s) as outlined above. However, the proceeds of the floating charge do not rank ahead of the super preferential and preferential creditors and these preferential creditors must be discharged in full prior to passing the proceeds of the realised "floating" assets to the debenture holder.

Examples of floating charge assets may be assets such as unspecified machinery, stock and or debtors of the company.

Further matters necessary for consideration here are:

- The receiver's costs and expenses are apportioned between those attributable to the realisation of fixed and floating assets respectively.

- Where the receiver is aware of any surplus on assets to be realised under a floating charge he is obliged to seek to agree the super preferential and preferential creditors at the earliest opportunity.

- Whether there are outstanding lease creditors with first rights to payment on the realisation of floating charge assets.

Receiver is appointed under a floating charge

Where a receiver is appointed under a floating charge, section 98 CA 1963 provides that the receiver must discharge the proceeds of the assets in order of priority as set out in section 285 CA1963 and distribute the surplus of the realisation to the debenture holder.

Surplus funds arising following realisations

In circumstances where surplus funds remain following the discharge of the fixed charge holder from the proceeds of assets and no floating charge exists, case law has ruled that these funds should be passed back to the company and not used directly to discharge the preferential creditors.

The receiver's role and functions

The receiver has many roles and responsibilities and the principal ones are as follows:

- act within the powers as outlined by the debenture deed

- take possession of the charged assets, to realise those assets and discharge the debt owing to the debenture/ charge holder

- collect and secure all property charged by the debenture and to take all and any proceedings in the name of the company or otherwise as may be necessary for that purpose

- continue to operate a business where the receiver believes that this will maximise the value of the company's assets with a view to selling the business as a going concern or sell part of the business and wind down the remaining business

- exercise care in disposing of company property (the receiver has a duty to obtain the best price reasonably obtainable for the asset being sold)

- to make arrangements or compromises that are in the best interests of the debenture holder

- when appointed under a floating charge, the receiver has a duty to pay the preferential creditors in priority to the debenture/charge holder

- under the 1990 legislation, a receiver is required to give 14 days' notice

under section 172(3) to all creditors where he or she intends to sell a non-cash asset of the company (defined in section 29 CA 1990 £50,000 or 10% of the net assets of the company and not less than £1,000) to a former officer of the company.

- it is appropriate for the receiver to seek and obtain good legal advice on his rights and obligations following his appointment. Ultimately, the debenture or charge document outlines the powers of the receiver. However, case law would indicate that directors and members of the company maintain rights and responsibilities, even following the appointment.

 Considerations following an appointment

Having taken possession of the asset(s) subject to the charge, the receiver **must** carry out the following tasks:

- arrange adequate insurance on the asset(s). In the majority of instances the appointment of a receiver or liquidator invalidates the company's insurance with immediate effect.

- He should notify the company's:
  - directors and secretary
  - employees
  - bank
  - lease/hire purchase creditors
  - solicitors
  - suppliers
  - creditors
  - agents
  - debtors

if the receiver is to continue to trade the business, he will be obliged to consider all retention of title claims, landlord issues, etc.

the receiver must ensure that all correspondence that issues contains the notation "In Receivership".

Timelines and Deadlines

The appointment of a receiver must be published, within seven days of the appointment, in:

- one daily newspaper circulating in the district where the registered office of the company is situated

- *An Iris Oifigiúil* (Government Publication)

The above tasks are usually carried out by the appointing institution's legal advisors.

Together with the above, a receiver is also required to deliver a **Notice of Appointment** to the Registrar of Companies within 14 days of the appointment.

If a receiver is appointed over the whole, or substantially whole, of the property of the company, the receiver must immediately send notice of his appointment to the company. The company is then obliged to file a statement of affairs of the company within 14 days after receipt of this notice. The statement of affairs is to be verified by an affidavit of at least one of the company's directors.

 # Closing a receivership

The receiver's appointment is concluded:

- when the debt owing to the debenture/charge holder is repaid, or

- when the assets over which he has been appointed have been fully realised or disposed of.

Once the matters outlined directly above have been finalised, the receiver should seek a formal deed of discharge from the debenture/charge holder. This document is then filed in the Companies' Registration Office (CRO) formally ending the receiver's involvement.

As with all assignments, it is incumbent upon the receiver and his advisors to ensure that all the required documents relating to the receivership process have been concluded. Examples of these are:

- All receivership tax returns and payments (where obliged) have been filed with the Revenue Commissioners.

- Where a debenture or charge has been satisfied in full, the required notice of satisfaction has been filed with the CRO.

- All receiver abstracts (Form 57 – cash accounts) have been completed and filed in the CRO.

- Together with his final abstract, the receiver is obliged to file a note as to the insolvent nature or otherwise of the company at the conclusion of the receivership. It is important to note for any accountant advising a company at the end of a receivership that this statement on the solvency of the company is available to the ODCE.

- Any contracts, agreements, legal actions, etc., that the receiver entered into during the course of the receivership have concluded.

- The receiver obtains a deed of discharge from the appointee and a copy of this document is filed with the CRO.

- A receiver and manager must also send notice to the directors of the company that responsibility for the company has passed back to its officers and return any company books and records to them.

- The receiver as a means of professional courtesy should also outline their responsibilities as directors to affect the winding up of the company (where applicable).

- While not obligatory, it remains good practice for the receiver to notify the Director of Corporate Enforcement that their appointment as receiver has ended.

 ## Case Study – *Example of Issues Arising*

Tom Kavanagh was appointed as a receiver and manager under a first fixed and floating charge to a large construction firm. The company had substantial preferential and unsecured creditors at the time of the appointment.

The company possessed a number of properties, had considerable amounts of machinery and a sizeable debtors' ledger.

Property

The receiver's legal advisors undertook a complete review of the properties encompassed by the charge. Following the review it transpired that:

- one property was partly built on land owned and charged to a different financial institution which significantly reduced its marketability and as a result its realisable value

- a second property was incorrectly registered in the land registry and resulted in a delay in excess of 24 months whilst the boundary was redrawn and re-registered.

The receiver also came into possession of two significant development sites. It was initially considered that the two sites in question were subject to a floating charge.

On reviewing matters, it transpired that contracts for sale had been agreed with a third party prior to his appointment.

Following his obtaining an independent valuation on these two sites, the receiver believed that the sale price of the sites were somewhat undervalued and sought to be released from the obligation to close the contracts.

Following a review of relevant case law, the advice received was such that the receiver was obliged to complete the contracts, as it was considered that they had been entered into in good faith at the time of signing contracts.

Following the completion of the sales and the receipt of proceeds of the two sites, the receiver instructed his legal advisors to review the specific charges under which they fell as, having reviewed the wording in the paperwork, it was considered that the wording on the charge documents appeared somewhat ambiguous.

The receiver instructed his advisors to seek Senior Counsel's opinion on this matter, and the advice received outlined that, while ambiguous, consideration needed to be given to the intention of the party when drawing up the charge, i.e. was it the intention to create a fixed charge on the properties? The opinion received was such that the intention had been to create a fixed charge.

The receiver proceeded to write to the Revenue Commissioners, outlining his advice on this matter and asking their consideration on the advice from Senior Counsel.

Having reviewed and taken advice on the matter, Revenue indicated their agreement with the interpretation and the proceeds of sale were allocated under a fixed charge and used to discharge the liability of the appointee.

(This example underlines the importance of competent legal advice when dealing with charge documents and property.)

Plant and Machinery

The receiver undertook a review of all plant and machinery following his appointment.

There were a large number of items that were subject to lease finance. An independent valuation of the financed assets confirmed that the lease liability exceeded the value of the assets. The receiver returned those assets to the respective leasing companies and arranged to dispose of the remaining plant and equipment in his possession.

On his appointment, there was also a considerable amount of plant and machinery on various sites the company was in the process of completing. With the agreement of the employer certain sites were cleared and items returned to the company's headquarters for disposal.

However, under clauses contained within the standard RIAI contract of employment, the employer is entitled by virtue of the company being placed in receivership to determine the contract and also to exercise a lien on plant and equipment of the contractor until the completion of the contract by an alternative contractor. On one significant contract following its determination, the employer notified the receiver and his advisors that they were exercising such a lien, thereby preventing the immediate return of the plant and machinery on site.

In circumstances such as this it is the receiver's responsibility to attempt to:

- obtain a written agreement on what items, subject to the receiver's appointment, remain on site

- obtain confirmation that the employer insures these items until such time as they are returned

- indemnify the receiver or his agents/successors from any liability howsoever caused by this equipment when in the possession of the employer

- obtain agreement on notification of the release of the equipment

- notify the employer of any claims for leased assets and inform the leasing company of the situation

- notify the employer of any claims under Retention of Title for items on site for which the liability has not been discharged.

The receiver should also ensure that he has informed his insurers of the position regarding all sites and assets under which he was appointed.

Ultimately, the receiver retrieved and disposed of the plant and equipment.

Contracts/Debtors

The majority of the construction contracts were determined following the appointment of the receiver. However, a number of employers were willing to allow the receiver to continue to complete the remaining works on a number of projects.

In order for this to occur, the receiver and his legal advisors needed to satisfy themselves that the charges under which he was appointed allowed the receiver to:

- borrow money to maximise realisations

- enter into contracts with third parties

- register for various taxes including VAT and RCT.

The receiver proceeded to complete one full housing estate development. This involved the marketing and sale of a number of properties, together with completing a significant amount of snagging works. This ultimately resulted in the receipt of significant sums of retention monies from developers and local authority housing schemes.

One particular item of note arises here in that the receiver should be aware that, on almost all occasions, local authority contracts differ from individual standard The Royal Institute of the Architects of Ireland "RIAI" contracts, in that there exists a clause allowing a right of set off from one contract to another where monies are owed by the contractor to the local authority.

Frequently Asked Questions

Q) Why appoint a receiver instead of a liquidator?

A) A receiver has a different role than that of a liquidator. Where a liquidator's obligation is to the benefit of all creditors, a receiver is appointed by one particular creditor and has powers over specified assets (although these may be wholly or substantially all of the assets of the company).

Q) The receivership is at an end and my client is no longer involved in the business. Does my client have any further obligations?

A) If the company is insolvent, there is an obligation to wind up the company whether or not the receivership has been concluded.

Q) Who can act as a receiver?

A) While there are no specific requirements as to who may act as a receiver, it is normally an accountant or member of the legal profession.

Under sections 314 and 315 Companies Act 1963 certain individuals are excluded from acting as receiver:

- a body corporate

- an undischarged bankrupt

- a person who has within a period of 12 months prior to the commencement of the receivership been an officer or a servant of the company

- a parent, spouse, brother, sister or child of an officer of the company

- a person who is a partner or in the employment of an officer of the company

Q) Is there a major advantage in appointing a receiver for the debenture/charge holder?

A) Yes. The appointment of a receiver gives the charge holder the immediate opportunity to take control of the charged assets and eliminate any further exposure or risk as a result of the ongoing default of the borrower.

Q) My clients believe that the debenture/charge holder has acted prematurely in appointing a receiver, is there anything that can be done?

A) There is a time limit of 72 hours in which the company can petition for the protection of the High Court and seek to have an examiner appointed. The 72 hours includes weekends and bank holidays. Failing that, a direct legal challenge to the validity of the appointment is an option. This is, however, less likely to succeed if the conditions that allow for the appointment of a receiver have occurred.

Q) Who pays the receiver?

A) The costs of the receivership process are paid out of the realisation of assets secured under the fixed or floating charge.

Note: The onus is on the receiver to maintain an accurate record of his time on the project identifying the appropriate time costs of realisations under the different type of charges.

For example, where a receiver is appointed over a fixed charge (relating to a property) and a floating charge relating to debtors, the receiver must only seek reimbursement for the time spent collecting the debts from the debtors and not the property. Equally, costs associated with the sale of the property cannot be paid from the collections from debtors. Fees charged against the realisation of book debts are usually approved in advance of payment by the fixed charge holder.

Q) Does the receiver need to deal with employee claims?

A) Depending upon the nature of the appointment (receiver, or receiver and manager) it is normal for the receiver to address and deal with the claims of the employees where, by virtue of his appointment, the employees' contracts are terminated. The receiver completes the employees' statutory entitlement forms and processes these through the Department of Enterprise, Trade and Employment.

Q) Does the appointment of a receiver lead to the termination of all employees?

A) The appointment of a receiver does not automatically lead to the termination of contracts with employees. Though it is normal where the company is ceasing to trade that the employees are let go and their entitlements are processed by the receiver's staff through the Department of Enterprise, Trade and Employment, there have been instances and case law which have found that, where the business was subsequently sold within a short time period and begins to trade again, the employees do have an entitlement to reinstatement.

Situations can occur where a potential purchaser does not wish to take on certain employees of a company, for whatever reason, and there have been cases where a receiver has made all employees redundant and the new purchaser immediately has hired back only those employees they wished to employ. The receiver and his legal advisors should always carefully

consider their actions in this regard and ensure that the sale document for the business indemnifies the receiver from any actions that may result from employees whose contracts have been terminated.

Q) What obligations does a receiver have to unsecured creditors?

A) The receiver acts on behalf of the debenture/charge holder and is obligated to obtain the best price for those charged assets. The receiver is not generally obliged to deal with the claims of unsecured creditors. The exception is in the case of unsecured creditors having valid retention of title claims on property or assets that the receiver is intending to realise.

Q) Is there a requirement on the receiver to file a report to the Director of Corporate Enforcement?

A) In a receivership, there is no requirement to report to the Director of Corporate Enforcement, or any obligation to bring a restriction application against any of the company's directors. The receiver is, however, bound by other forms of reporting requirements such as:

- an obligation under section 58 CLEA 2001 for failure to maintain proper books and records and

- section 192 CA 1990 as amended by section 73 CLEA 2001, where the receiver is obliged to make a report to the Director of Corporate Enforcement and the Director of Public Prosecutions when he or she has reasonable grounds for believing that a member has committed an indictable offence under the Companies Acts in the course of the receivership.

Q) Is it possible for a receiver to resign?

A) Section 177 of the Companies

(Amendment) Act 1990 (C(A)A 1990) provides that a receiver may resign his or her position after giving one month's notice to the holders of:

- any floating charges over all or any part of the property of the company

- any fixed charges over all or any part of the property of the company

- the company or its liquidator.

A receiver appointed by the court may only resign with the permission of the court.

Q) What happens when the debenture/charge holder is paid in full?

A) Following the repayment of the debenture/charge holder, any surplus funds are paid back to the company and it is for the company to take the appropriate steps at that time. This would usually but not always mean seeking the appointment of a liquidator.

Q) Can the receiver sue the directors of the company?

A) Where a receiver believes that assets under his charge may have been misappropriated he can apply to the High Court for orders to:

- return company assets

- freeze directors' assets

- take other appropriate measures to assist in the receivership process.

A receiver can also issue proceedings against officers of the company under:

- section 139 CA 1963

- reckless trading legislation pursuant to section 297 CA 1963

- section 150 CA 1990 (restriction proceedings)

- section 160 CA 1990 (disqualification proceedings).

Q) How long does the receivership process take?

A) Receiverships can vary significantly from one assignment to another depending on many varying factors such as the:

- type/size of property involved and its location,

- clean title to the property / properties in question,

- type of business and its saleability in the marketplace,

- size and age of the company's debtors ledger.

Typically, a receivership takes between nine and 24 months. However, certain assignments can last much longer.

Q) How does the appointment of a receiver affect my client's personal guarantee on the assets under charge?

A) It is usual for the appointee to place a stay on any proceedings seeking to enforce such personal security pending the outcome of the receivership process. However, where it is clear that there is likely to be a substantial shortfall in the realisations versus the outstanding debt, it is prudent of the debenture/charge holder to instigate proceedings for any likely shortfall in the recovery.

Q) The deed of appointment has not yet been filed in the CRO. Is the receiver validly appointed?

A) There is a time limit of 14 days for the appropriate documentation to be filed in the CRO. The deed of appointment is effective when signed by the appropriate parties.

Chapter >> 4

Court Liquidations

Chapter 4 Overview

What is a court liquidation?

An insolvent company can be wound up voluntarily or through the court.

Simply put, a court liquidation is the winding up process by which, under the supervision of the High Court and the Office of the High Court Examiner, the following occurs:

- A liquidator is appointed to an insolvent company

- that company's affairs are investigated

- its assets are realised

- creditors are paid in a strict legal preference, and ultimately

- the company is legally dissolved.

Legislation, and guidance from Chartered Accountants Ireland

Court liquidations are dealt with comprehensively in the Companies Act 1963 (CA 1963) and Companies Act 1990 (CA 1990). Of particular relevance is section 214 CA 1963.

Statements of Insolvency Practice are issued by Chartered Accountants Ireland to insolvency practitioners with a view to maintaining standards by setting out required practice and harmonising members' approach to particular aspects of insolvency. The purpose of Statements of

Insolvency Practice is to set out basic principles and essential procedures with which insolvency practitioners are required to comply. In terms of court liquidations, the following are of relevance:

- S191208: Anti-money Laundering for Insolvency Practitioners

- S2B: Liquidator's investigation

- S7B: Preparation of receipts and payments

- S9B: Remuneration of insolvency officeholders

- S11B: The Handling of Funds

- S13B: Acquisition of Assets of Insolvent Companies

- S15B: Dealing with employee claims

- S17B: Committee of Inspection

- S18B: Reporting by Liquidators

When is a court liquidation suitable/ appropriate?

A court liquidation differs from a creditors' voluntary liquidation (CVL) in that there is no meeting of creditors to wind up the company; there is no need to give the statutory 10 days' notice; and a delay in the appointment of a liquidator can be avoided by the appointment of a provisional liquidator.

A petition to wind up a company and have a provisional liquidator appointed is a valuable tool in circumstances where there is a risk that the business or asset(s) of the company may be substantially devalued due to the issuing of notices to creditors and/or the cessation of the company's trade during the 10-day notice period applicable to a CVL.

An application to appoint a provisional liquidator is most usual when the company, its shareholders or its directors' petition the court for the winding up of the company. A **creditor** can, however, seek the immediate appointment of a provisional liquidator, though the petitioning creditor must show compelling reasons for the appointment.

There is an increasing number of petitions being made to the High Court on behalf of creditors who believe the company to be insolvent as it cannot pay its debt to that creditor. This must be caveated immediately as it is very important to note that the payment can only be obtained by way of receiving a distribution (dividend) as a result of the liquidation process and there is no guarantee that there will be funds available for such a distribution. The High Court has strict criteria for

petitioning to place a company into liquidation, and will **not** entertain a petition that appears solely to be a debt collection method or threat to obtain payment. The Court may make a petitioning creditor liable for the costs of the petition if the Court believes that the petition was inappropriate.

Who are the key parties involved?

The process of placing a company into liquidation by way of a court order is discussed further below. However, the main parties involved in the process are as follows:

- petitioner (be it the company itself, a creditor, a director or shareholder)

- petitioner's solicitors

- petitioner's barrister

- provisional/official liquidator's solicitor

- provisional/official liquidator.

Recent statistics

In 2008, court liquidations accounted for approximately 11% of all liquidations. The chart below shows the number of court liquidations in the Republic of Ireland in 2007, 2008 and 2009 (to end August). As with all insolvency types, the numbers of court liquidations have increased due partly to greater financial difficulties in the economy and a propensity towards litigation in difficult times.

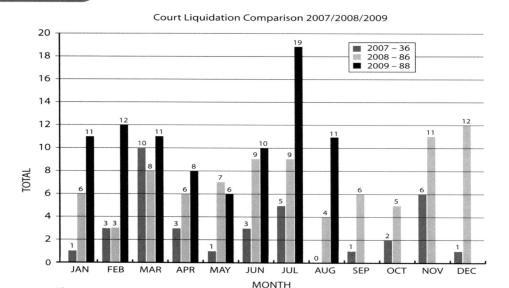

Court Liquidation Comparison 2007/2008/2009

| 2007 – 36 |
| 2008 – 86 |
| 2009 – 88 |

(Courtesy: www.insolvencyjournal.ie)

The process of a court liquidation

When a creditor is seeking to wind up a debtor, before bringing a petition to wind up the debtor, it would be usual for the creditor, unless specific circumstances have arisen, to have exhausted every avenue to collect the debt owed.

Any creditor of a company can petition to wind up a debtor company provided their debt is in excess of the High Court limit of €1,269.74 (although given the costs involved in instigating a court liquidation, the sum involved would need to be considerably higher to even entertain this option).

A petition is brought under section 214 CA 1963. Under this section it must be proved that a company is unable to discharge its debts as they fall due. A creditor issues a 21-day letter of demand to the debtor company. The 21-day letter of demand should be served on the debtor company's registered office. Should the debtor company fail to discharge the debt within this timeframe, this is accepted as prima facie evidence of the debtor company's insolvency.

Thereafter, details of the petition **must** be advertised in the national press. It is important to note that the High Court is highly unlikely to place a company into liquidation if notification of the petition has not been advertised.

In circumstances where the company itself, is the petitioner, a court liquidation is initiated through a petition after the passing of a resolution of the board that the company be placed into liquidation and an official or provisional liquidator appointed.

As outlined above, in certain circumstances the High Court will first appoint a provisional liquidator and make a decision on the appointment of an **official**

liquidator on the full hearing of the petition and receipt of a report from the provisional liquidator.

Below is a list of **circumstances in which a company may be wound up by the court under section 213 CA 1963:**

▦ the company is unable to pay its debts

▦ the company has by special resolution resolved that the company be wound up by the court

▦ default is made in delivering the statutory report to the Company Registrar or in holding the statutory meeting

▦ the company does not commence its business within a year from its incorporation or suspends its business for a whole year

▦ the number of members is reduced, in the case of a private company, below two, or, in the case of any other company, below seven

▦ the court is of the opinion that it is just and equitable that the company should be wound up

▦ the court is satisfied that the company's affairs are being conducted, or the powers of the directors are being exercised, in a manner oppressive to any member or in disregard of his interests as a member and that, despite the existence of an alternative remedy, winding up would be justified in the general circumstances of the case. The court may dismiss a petition to wind up under this paragraph if it is of opinion

that proceedings under section 205 would, in all the circumstances, be more appropriate. In effect, this means that the High Court may in certain circumstances, even if other legal remedies are available, place a company into liquidation if the court believes that the company operated in an unfair manner towards some or all of its shareholders.

Drafting Petition Papers

The drafting of petition papers is, in general, carried out by a solicitor with appropriate insolvency expertise and may take a number of days for completion. The petition papers should outline the following:

● a brief history of the company to include its function

● a brief analysis of the company's financial performance over the past three to five years

● a description of the problems being faced by the company, which warrant the appointment of a liquidator

● a conclusion as to why the company should be granted an order from the court to be wound up.

The petition papers should also be accompanied by a grounding affidavit and verifying affidavit signed by the petitioner or a director of the petitioner. This affidavit verifies the information contained within the petition, the background of the company, the status of the company (shareholding) and details of its insolvency.

Along with the affidavits and petition papers it is usual that the following are exhibited:

- special resolution to wind up the company (if applicable)

- any key documentation/agreements of relevance (potentially or otherwise) to the court's decision

- certificate of incorporation

- an up-to-date company printout

- the most recent annual return

- the most recent financial statements of the company

- letter of consent from the proposed liquidator to act as provisional liquidator and/or official liquidator, if appointed.

The liquidator is also required to submit an **affidavit of fitness** sworn by a solicitor. This affidavit confirms the liquidator's status as a responsible insolvency practitioner and suitable person to act as liquidator.

The hearing of the petition

Following submission of the petition papers and affidavits, the case is listed on the Chancery listing of the High Court. This list is usually heard on Monday mornings during Court term, and the list is available from the legal diary section of the Court Services Website, **www.courts.ie**.

Once all statutory obligations regarding notification and advertisement are in order,

the papers are reviewed by the sitting judge who will then make the decision on whether to appoint a provisional or official liquidator.

If a provisional liquidator is appointed, it is normal for the judge to grant a return date in approximately two to three weeks' time, at which stage the provisional liquidator is required to submit a report to the High Court.

At this hearing, and following a review of the provisional liquidator's report, the judge may grant the appointment of an official liquidator if the company has failed to address the issues outlined in the petition papers.

On the appointment of the official liquidator, the case is then listed for its first consideration hearing in the Examiner's Court, which is generally three to six weeks after the official liquidator's appointment. The official liquidator is required to issue a report to the High Court at this hearing, updating the High Court on all matters relating to the case. The Examiner's Court list is usually heard on Monday mornings during Court term and the list is again available from the legal diary section of the Court Services Website, **www.courts.ie**.

Immediately prior to the first consideration of the case by the High Court, the High Court Examiner will seek a notice to proceed meeting with the official liquidator and his legal advisors.

The Office of the High Court Examiner and their role is discussed below in the next section.

The role of the High Court Examiner

The High Court Examiner acts as an intermediary between an official liquidator and the judge. Any documentation which is to be put before a judge is first reviewed by the Court Examiner.

Shortly after the appointment as official liquidator a meeting is held between the Court Examiner, the official liquidator and the official liquidator's legal advisors. At this meeting the official liquidator is required to furnish the following:

1. Notice to Proceed

(being effectively a request by the official liquidator to carry out their duties as outlined in the appointing Court order)

2. Letter to the High Court Examiner stating:

- whether or not an examiner was previously appointed or the company was under the protection of the Court

- whether or not any orders were made between the presentation of the petition and the making of the winding up order

- whether or not any orders were made after the winding up order

3. Completed Draft Bond or, alternatively, an affidavit verifying the professional indemnity insurance cover for insolvency services and seeking an order of the court to dispense with the necessity for a bond. By way of explanation, the bond is effectively insurance cover to prevent error or impropriety by the liquidator or their staff.

4. An up-to-date company search on the company in liquidation

5. Copy of the Statement of Affairs unlike CVL, this is a sworn document

6. Initial Report prepared by official liquidator

7. Affidavit of Service of Winding up Order on:

- the company

- The Registrar of Companies

- The Sheriff

- Bank of Ireland (College Green)

- The directors who have been directed to file the statement of affairs

8. Original statutory advertisements

9. Completed authorisation form to open a bank account

10. Completed authorisation form to appoint a solicitor

(List courtesy of the Office of the High Court Examiner)

Bank Account

The Court Examiner is an authorised signatory on all court liquidation accounts. Therefore, all cheques or transfers issued from an official liquidator's accounts are reviewed and countersigned by the Court Examiner. In the normal run of events, a cheque is forwarded to the Court Examiner with relevant back-up documentation, reviewed, signed and returned to the official liquidator for distribution to the beneficiary.

Subject to Court permission the liquidator can, however, obtain a float account on which the Court Examiner's signature is not required.

Vouching of accounts

At the notice to proceed meeting, the Court Examiner will set a date for vouching of the official liquidator's cash accounts. This process involves the official liquidator attending a meeting with the Court Examiner during which each transaction through the official liquidation bank account is cross-referenced to the appropriate paperwork.

Should a debtor balance have been comprised during the liquidation process the Court Examiner will seek an adequate explanation for the write-down in the debt. These write-downs are also reported to the High Court in the official liquidator's court report and eventually an order must be sought to confirm the write off.

The adjudicating of claims

Should an official liquidator be in a position to discharge a dividend to the preferential and/or unsecured creditors of a company, the Court Examiner is required to adjudicate each creditor's claim. This can be a lengthy process as each invoice submitted by a creditor is reviewed to ensure that the claim relates to a pre-liquidation period and that the amounts included are correct.

Again, once all dividend cheques have been drafted they require the signature of both the official liquidator and the Court Examiner.

Issuing the Final Certificate

When an official liquidation has been completed and is in its final stages, a court application is made to formally discharge the official liquidator. Following the final payments from the official liquidator's bank accounts, the final bank statement showing a nil balance is forwarded to the Court Examiner. The Court Examiner will then issue the final certificate, which formally allows the official liquidator to lodge his final forms with the Companies Registration Office (CRO) and have the company dissolved.

 ## The role and function of the court-appointed liquidator

When an order is made appointing a provisional liquidator, this order will grant the provisional liquidator certain powers. It is vitally important that a provisional liquidator does not act outside the powers granted to him as, if he does:

- the provisional liquidator will have breached an order of the High Court

- the actions outside of the granted powers may be reversed and the provisional liquidator made liable for any costs incurred

- such a breach may be considered grounds to remove the provisional liquidator or prevent their appointment as official liquidator.

The role of an official liquidator is predominantly the same as a liquidator appointed by way of a creditors' voluntary liquidation (CVL) as detailed in **Chapter 2**. This includes the obligations under section 56 CLEA 2001.

Key differences to a creditors' voluntary liquidation

There are a number of differences between a CVL and a court liquidation. The main differences are outlined below.

- **Committee of Inspection**
  In a CVL the creditors have an opportunity to appoint a committee of inspection at the meeting of creditors held to formally appoint a liquidator. In a court liquidation there is no such meeting. However, the court may order that the liquidator hold a meeting of the creditors with the express purpose of appointing a committee of inspection. While Committees are commonplace in CVLs, they are currently rare in court liquidations.

- **Court Examiner**
  The role of the Court Examiner is specific only to court liquidations. The Court Examiner's role has been detailed above. The Court Examiner Office is located on Phoenix Street North, Smithfield, Dublin 1. For further information, see **www.courts.ie**.

- **Reports to Courts**
  A liquidator appointed by court order will report to the High Court in three manners:
  1] communication to the Office of the High Court Examiner
  2] through the liquidator's appointed barrister, who may address the judge with any important matters he or she believes need to be mentioned
  3] written reports to court.

- **Statement of Affairs**
  As outlined in earlier chapters, in a CVL the directors are required to prepare a statement of affairs for presentation at the meeting of creditors. In the case of a court liquidation, the High Court grants an order requiring the directors to submit a statement of affairs, generally within four to six weeks of the date on which the petition is granted The statement of affairs in a court liquidation is a sworn document.

  In general, the High Court will accept a delay in submitting the directors' sworn statement of affairs if there is a valid reason for the delay. If there is no valid reason, failure to submit the statement of affairs is in breach of a High Court order and, although rare, can result in an order committing the director(s) to prison.

The directors may request that the company's accountant assist in the completion of the statement of affairs. The accountant may apply to have his or her fees **paid** through the liquidation provided that the following steps are followed:

- there are funds available to discharge any fee for the preparation of the statement of affairs.

- the accountant gives a quotation for fees in advance in writing to the official liquidator.

- once the figure has been agreed, the official liquidator must make the accountant aware that getting paid will take time, as the cheque will have to be approved and countersigned by the Court Examiner.

- when it comes to billing, the accountant should discuss his or her actual bill with the official liquidator before it is finalised.

- the accountant should forward his invoice addressed to the company in liquidation and **must** supply supporting time analysis sheets.

- all the correspondence between the liquidator and the accountant (including memos of telephone conversations) should be forwarded to the Court Examiner's office with the cheque for the Court Examiner's countersignature.

The standard format for a court liquidation statement of affairs is available from the Companies Registration Office Website, **www.cro.ie**.

- **Requirement of a Solicitor**
  In a court liquidation, it is necessary to employ the services of an **experienced insolvency solicitor** to guide and assist the court-appointed official liquidator through the various legal requirements, dealing with the Court Examiner, advising on the powers of a provisional liquidator and drafting of various affidavits.

- **Companies' Registration Office**
  In a court liquidation, it is not necessary to call an Annual General Meeting on the anniversary of the official liquidator's appointment. It is also only necessary to file a **Form 22/23** cash account with the CRO on an annual basis following the second anniversary of the official liquidator's appointment.

 Closing a court liquidation

As with a CVL, similar notifications must be made and clearances received before moving to close a court liquidation. Once these matters are finalised:

- The official liquidator must make an application to the Court in order to finalise a court liquidation.

- Prior to the hearing of same, a detailed report of the progress of the liquidation since commencement, together with supporting affidavits and motions, must be approved by the High Court Examiner.

- Once approved, the final application will be set for hearing and any notice parties must be advised of the final application and the date set for the hearing.

Case Study –
Intel Limited

Intel Limited was a substantial freight forwarding and logistics company based out of Knocktopher in County Kilkenny. The company had been incorporated on 1 January 1986 and had traded successfully for many years before running into financial difficulty during 2001 and 2002 as a result of bad debts, over-expansion and escalating costs.

Reasons for the appointment of provisional liquidator

Ken Fennell was appointed as provisional liquidator to the company on foot of a petition presented by the company on 16 August 2002. The application to appoint a provisional liquidator was predominantly grounded on the following:

Safeguarding the business of the company

- The company's core business was potentially profitable and therefore the sale of same was a genuine possibility if a provisional liquidator was appointed to continue the business. This business would be lost if the company ceased to trade during the 10-day notice period required for a creditors' voluntary liquidation.

- There were substantial amounts of goods on site and in transit for the company's customers and, if a provisional liquidator was not in place to ensure the delivery of the goods, the company's debtors' ledger and customer base would be detrimentally affected.

- The c_____
  withdraw_____
  and it was i_____
  would be unabl_____
  other arrangements_____
  unable to continue to _____

Safeguarding the assets of t___ company

- The company had a large fleet of trailers, which were in various locations across Europe and which would need to be secured immediately or there was a risk they would be lost.

- Even in the short term, the business and potential value of the company's Italian subsidiary would be detrimentally impacted should its Irish trading partner/parent company cease to trade for any length of time.

Why not appoint an Examiner?

The company's debtors were subject to a finance agreement and, given the expected extent of the company's bad debts and the withdrawal of certain finance facilities, it was believed that the company would not be in a position to finance operations during the 70 days (potentially 100 days) of the examination. The immediate appointment of a provisional liquidator allowed trade to continue on a limited basis while the business and goodwill of the company was marketed.

Outcome of the appointment of the provisional liquidator

- The company's goodwill and customer base were sold for €75,000.

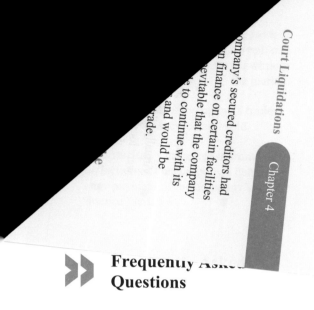

...ompany's secured creditors had ...n finance on certain facilities ...evitable that the company ...e to continue with its ...r and would be ...rade.

Deliveries were maintained.

The Italian subsidiary's trade continued and the company's shareholding in the Italian company was sold for €225,000.

There were dividend payments to all classes of creditors, including 100% dividends to the preferential and floating charge holders.

►► Frequently Asked Questions

Petitioner's/Company's Perspective

Q) Am I, as a director of the company, required to appear and address the court when petitioning to wind up my company?

A) If the directors are the petitioners, a company director is generally in attendance at the initial hearing. The director is required to submit an affidavit; however, it is highly unusual for the High Court to request the director to verbally address the court as all issues are generally dealt with by the company's legal representative/barrister.

Q) A debtor of my company has failed to pay within our agreed 30-day credit limit. Can I issue section 214 proceedings immediately?

A) Prior to issuing section 214 proceedings, it is usually advisable that you have first pursued other avenues in an attempt to secure payment. In order to

have the best chance of securing judgment, it is also advisable to retain all written requests for payment and exhibit them in the section 214 application, supported by, if available, confirmation of the sums owed. This effectively allows the High Court to understand that you have made every attempt to realise the debtor and that issuing section 214 proceedings is realistically your last option.

Q) I am proceeding with a section 214 action against a company. Who appoints the provisional/official liquidator?

A) Prior to taking the section 214 action, it is advisable to have a nominee provisional/ official liquidator in place who is capable of taking the assignment. This is something that can be arranged through direct contact with a firm of insolvency practitioners or through your legal advisors.

Q) My section 214 application has been successful. When will I receive the money I am owed?

A) Being the petitioning creditor does not give the creditor an elevated position in the liquidation. If you are successful in a section 214 application your debt is held in the same regard as all other unsecured creditors. Generally, all creditors of a company are informed of the likelihood of a dividend payment within six to 12 months of the commencement of a liquidation.

Q) I have incurred substantial legal fees in securing my section 214 application. When will these fees be discharged?

A) If sufficient funds are available in the liquidation, the petitioners' fees rank ahead of all other creditors. It can take up to 12 months for these fees to be discharged depending on asset realisations. Court approval is also needed to discharge the fees.

Q) As a director of the company, I have petitioned to have a provisional liquidator appointed to enable the business to continue. May I still continue in my role as a director of the company?

A) Upon appointment of an official liquidator, your powers as a director of the company cease. Should the company continue to trade while in liquidation, the provisional/official liquidator may ask permission of the court to retain your services to assist in the running of the company.

Q) Is there a requirement for an official liquidator to report on my actions to the ODCE?

A) A provisional/official liquidator is required to report to the Director of Corporate Enforcement in the form of a section 56 report within six months of his or her official appointment.

Q) I have been ordered to prepare a statement of affairs. What are the implications for me if this is not prepared?

A) Failure to prepare the statement of affairs is a breach of an order of the High Court. Leaving aside the costs that could be awarded against you for the liquidator's own time and that of his legal advisors for having to pursue you to complete same, persistent failure may result in you being summonsed before the High Court and potentially being subject to an order of committal to prison.

Q) Is a court liquidation more expensive than a creditors' voluntary liquidation?

A) Unfortunately, the court process does give rise to higher costs than in a creditors' voluntary liquidation, due to the increased level of reporting, the increased involvement of legal advisors and counsel, coupled with court duties payable (being a statutory fee payable of 4% on net realisations received).

Accounting Practitioner's Perspective

Q) An official liquidator has been appointed to a client. What is the likelihood of my outstanding fees being discharged?

A) An auditor's fees rank as an unsecured creditor claim in the liquidation process. Generally, all creditors of a company are informed of the likelihood of a dividend payment within six to 12 months of the commencement of a liquidation.

Q) I am currently in the middle of auditing my client who has gone into liquidation. Should I finalise my audit?

A) There is no obligation on the auditor to finalise his or her audit. Should there be no dividend to the unsecured creditors, an auditor will not be paid for the completion of the work.

Q) I had retained books and records of my client while completing my audit. Should I retain these records?

A) These records should be forwarded to the provisional/official liquidator who has a responsibility to retain all books and records of the company for a period of up to six years.

Q) The directors of my client have been ordered by the High Court to submit a directors' statement of affairs. Can I be paid from the liquidation for preparing this documentation?

A) The directors are entitled to engage the services of an accountant for the preparation of the directors' estimated statement of affairs. Subject to the availability of funds, the fees incurred in preparing this document may be claimed through the liquidation upon agreement with the official liquidator (see page 64).

Q) My client, a director of a company now in liquidation, has expressed an interest in purchasing back the assets of the company now in liquidation. Is my client entitled to do so?

A) The sales of assets of a company to a director are covered under section 231(a) of the Companies Act 1963. It is necessary for the creditors to be given 14 days' notice of the sale of assets once the value of the assets exceeds certain limits.

Q) My client is owed €50,000 from a company in official liquidation. My client holds a retention/reservation of title claim and believes his products remain on-site. Can my client retrieve his goods?

A) If your client's products are on site and their retention/reservation of title claim is valid, the provisional / official liquidator will assist in the return of your client's products. Depending on the size of the case, this process can take between two to six weeks. Should your clients' goods not be available to the liquidator in their original form, your client's claim will rank as unsecured against the company.

Q) My client has been contacted by an official liquidator who has been granted authority to continue trading by the High Court. My client holds valid

retention/reservation of title over his products, which the official liquidator is proposing to use, will my client be paid for allowing the liquidator use this stock?

A) Providing your client's retention of title claim is valid, your client must be paid in full for the stock used during the period of the liquidation over which it has retained title.

Q) My client has been contacted by an official liquidator who intends to continue the business of the company in liquidation. The official liquidator has requested to purchase a quantity of stock, which he has informed me will be paid for in full, can my client be paid the liability for stock sold pre-liquidation also?

A) In circumstances where an official liquidator is continuing to trade, there will be a requirement to purchase stocks. The official liquidator is obliged to pay for such stocks. However, any liability arising as a result of the stocks purchased by the company pre-liquidation ranks as an unsecured claim and the official liquidator cannot discharge same without a court order.

Chapter ▶▶ 5

Members' Voluntary Liquidations

Chapter 5 Overview

What is a members' voluntary liquidation?

A members' voluntary liquidation is not actually a form of insolvency. It is a process by which a solvent company's affairs are wound down as follows:

- a liquidator is appointed to a solvent company

- that company's assets are realised

- creditors are paid in a strict legal preference

- the remaining sums available are distributed to shareholders/members, after deduction of capital gains tax, and

- Ultimately the company is legally dissolved

The members of a solvent company resolve by special resolution to wind up the company on the basis that the company will be able to pay its debts within 12 months of the passing of the resolution.

 ## Legislation

Companies Act 1963:

- Section 252 – publication of resolution to wind up voluntarily

- Section 253 – commencement of voluntary winding up

- Section 254 – effect of voluntary winding up on business and status of company

- Section 255 – avoidance of transfers of shares after commencement of voluntary winding up

- Section 256 – Statutory Declaration of Solvency in case of proposal to wind up voluntarily

- Section 257 – Provisions applicable to a members' voluntary winding up

- Section 258 – Power of the Company to appoint and fix remuneration of liquidators

- Section 259 – Power to fill vacancy in office of liquidator

- Section 260 – Power of liquidator to accept shares as consideration for sale of property of company

- Section 261 – Duty of the liquidator to call a meeting of creditors if he is of the opinion that the Company is unable to pay its debts

- Section 262 – Duty of liquidator to call general meeting at the end of the year

- Section 263 – Final Meeting and Dissolution

 ## When is a members' voluntary liquidation suitable/appropriate?

A members' voluntary liquidation (MVL) is suitable for a solvent company that has sufficient funds to pay its liabilities within 12 months of the commencement of the winding up process. It is generally used:

- by shareholders wishing to unlock their capital in a tax efficient manner

- to secure the orderly wind-down of a trading or dormant company

- to dispose of a company that has ceased trading

- to close down a subsidiary, within a group of companies, that has outlived its usefulness

- to wind down financial services companies and/or special purpose investment vehicles

- as an alternative to a strike-off

 ## Who are the key parties involved?

- **solicitor**
  prepares the documentation necessary to place the company into liquidation and also advises on any legal issues that may affect the progress of the liquidation

- **directors**
  responsible for preparing the **Declaration of Solvency**, which includes a statement of assets and liabilities of the company dated not more than three months before the declaration is made

- **auditor/accountant**
  prepares the documentation necessary to place the company into liquidation. The auditor/accountant first gives their consent to act as the independent person (as specifically outlined in the declaration of solvency) and then prepares the report of an independent person. The auditor/accountant will compile a statement of assets and liabilities for inclusion in the declaration. The auditor/accountant will also prepare statutory accounts if required by the CRO.

- **members/shareholders**
  meet to agree the resolutions to place the company into liquidation and to appoint a liquidator

 ## Recent statistics

Overleaf is a graph showing the number of members' voluntary liquidations from 2007 to Augsut 2009.

The consistently high level of MVLs, despite the downturn, may be more demonstrative of businesses being closed to avoid exposure to deteriorating markets than cases of effective tax planning seen during the boom times.

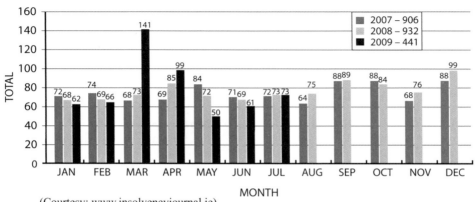

MVL Comparison 2007/2008/2009

Legend:
2007 – 906
2008 – 932
2009 – 441

(Courtesy: www.insolvencyjournal.ie)

 The process of a members' voluntary liquidation

Pre appointment

Convene a meeting of the board of directors to:

- authorise the convening of an Extraordinary General Meeting of the company to wind up the company as a members' voluntary winding up and to appoint a liquidator

- authorise the preparation of a declaration of solvency and arrange for an independent person to report on the declaration of solvency and consent to the issue of the declaration

- nominate a liquidator and arrange for the liquidator to give his or her consent to act as liquidator

Declaration of Solvency (Timelines and deadlines)

- a declaration of solvency is prepared by the directors of the company

- the directors make a sworn declaration that, having made a full inquiry into the affairs of the company, they have formed the opinion that the company will be able to pay its debts in full within a period **not exceeding** 12 months from the commencement of the winding up

- the Declaration of Solvency includes a statement of the assets and liabilities of the company made at the latest practical date before the declaration is made, and in any event not more than three months before the declaration is made. The statement of assets and liabilities that forms **"Part A"** of the declaration is supported by a Report of an Independent Person and Consent of an Independent Person, being **"Part B"** and **"Part C"** of the Declaration of Solvency, respectively

- the declaration must be signed by all or a majority of the directors (if more than two directors) consenting to the declaration and sworn by a practising solicitor or a commissioner for oaths preferably at least one day before the members' meeting to place the company into voluntary liquidation, or within 28 days in advance of the passing of a resolution to wind up the company. (In practice, the declaration is usually sworn by a solicitor at the board meeting.) In the event that the board meeting and the Extraordinary General Meeting of members (shareholders) are held on the same day, then the timing of the board meeting, declaration of solvency, report and consent of the independent person, will need to be inserted on to all documentation

- a declaration of solvency can be sworn in a foreign jurisdiction that is party to the Hague Convention. The declaration must be sworn before a person entitled to administer oaths for that jurisdiction and must be accompanied by a certificate of legalisation called an **apostile**, which confirms the capacity in which the person signing the document has acted and that the signature, seal or stamp of the person that the document bears, are certified. The apostile can be obtained from the designated authority for that jurisdiction

- the effective date for the declaration of solvency is the date the declaration is sworn

Report of 'Independent Person' (Part B)

- the independent person is a person that is qualified at the time of the report to be appointed, or to continue as auditor of the company

- the report must state that they have given their consent to the declaration of solvency being issued and that, in their opinion and to the best of the information and explanations given to them, the statutory declaration of the directors is reasonable

- the report of the independent person must be signed after the swearing of the declaration and within 14 days of the swearing

Consent of 'Independent Person' (Part C)

- the independent person has given and not withdrawn their written consent to the issue of the declaration of solvency with their report attached

- the consent of the independent person must also be signed after the swearing of the Declaration and within 14 days of the swearing

- it is important to note the contents of section 256(8) CA 1963, which, in essence, state that if it can be proved to the court's satisfaction that despite the declaration of solvency, the company is not able to pay its debts, the court may make any director who was party to the declaration personally liable for part or all of the debts of the company.

Extraordinary General Meeting (EGM)

- an EGM of members must take place within 28 days of making the declaration of solvency where a special resolution is passed to wind up the company followed by an ordinary resolution to appoint a liquidator

- a copy of the sworn declaration must be attached to the notices of the EGM that will issue to the members otherwise the declaration will have no effect

- the EGM can be held at less notice than the statutory notice period, provided the company obtain written consent to short notice of the EGM from the shareholders and the auditor

- in the event that the board meeting and the EGM are held on the same day, then the timing of the board meeting, declaration of solvency, report and consent of the independent person will need to be inserted on to all documentation

- the following resolutions are passed at the EGM:

  (a) to wind up the company as a members' voluntary winding up

  (b) to appoint a liquidator

  (c) To authorise the liquidator to distribute the whole or any part of the assets of the company amongst the members in specie if permitted by the memorandum and articles of association of the company

- the resolutions must be filed with the Companies' Registration Office (CRO) within 15 days of the date of the meeting

- the winding up is deemed to commence at the time of passing the special resolution for winding up

Documents required to commence the process

The following documents must be completed to commence the liquidation process:

1. minutes of board meeting

2. declaration of solvency

3. report of independent person

4. consent of independent person

5. notice of the EGM

6. general proxy for use at the EGM

7. consent to short notice of shareholders and auditors where the EGM is being held within the statutory notice period

8. minutes of the EGM

9. Form G1

10. Form G2

What happens once the liquidator has been appointed?

The company will cease to carry on its business, apart from business that may be required for the beneficial winding up. The corporate state and corporate powers of the company, unless otherwise stated by the company's articles of association, will continue until the company is dissolved after the completion of the liquidation.

The role and function of the liquidator

- arrange for statutory company secretarial documents to be filed with the CRO

- verify the location of statutory and accounting books and records

- notify all professional advisors of the liquidation and obtain the necessary clearances

- verify the value of assets of the company

- realise any assets

- verify the liabilities of the company

- place a notice in a national newspaper calling creditors to submit any claims against the company within a strict time frame

- pay all classes of creditors

- wind up the affairs of the company

- distribute the company's net assets amongst the shareholders in accordance with their percentage shareholding and the different entitlements owing to each class of shareholder in a winding up

- dissolve the company in accordance with the Companies Acts 1963–2006

- in accordance with section 261 CA 1963, if the liquidator is at any time of the opinion that the company will not be able to pay its debts in full within the period stated in the declaration, he or she must convene a meeting of creditors no later than the 14th day after the day on which he or she formed that opinion and shall present before the meeting a statement of the assets and liabilities of the company

- reconcile the last set of audited accounts to the Declaration of Solvency to ensure there are no material differences

Statutory Requirements

The liquidator of a company being wound up by way of a members' voluntary liquidation must address a number of statutory obligations as outlined below:

- the Declaration of Solvency (**Form E1/12**) must be filed with the CRO no later than the date of delivery to the CRO of the special resolution for the winding-up

- the Special Resolution (**Form G1**) and Ordinary Resolution (**Form G2**) must be lodged with the CRO within 15 days after passing the resolution to wind up the company

- a Notice of Appointment of Liquidator (**Form 39A/E2**) must be filed with the CRO within 14 days of appointment

- the resolution to wind up the company including the name and address of the liquidator must be advertised in the Government publication, *An Iris Oifigiúil,* within 14 days after passing the resolution

- if the liquidation exceeds 12 months, the liquidator must call an Annual General Meeting (AGM) of the company within at least three months from the anniversary of the commencement of the winding up

- the liquidator must present before the annual general meeting an account of the liquidator's acts and dealings during the preceding 12 months

- the liquidator must file with the CRO the liquidator's account of his or her dealings (**Form E3**) summary cash account within seven days of the AGM

- if the liquidation exceeds two years, the liquidator must call a second AGM and file a liquidator's affidavit and section 306 accounts, **Forms 22/23 (E4)** cash account within seven days of the AGM

- the liquidator must file **Form 22/23 (E4)** every six months thereafter

- when all issues relating to the liquidation have been resolved; the liquidator will call a final meeting of the company, file a return of the final winding up (**Form 13 (E6)**) and a statement of account of the liquidator's dealings that covers the full duration of the liquidation (**Form 14**)

- the company is dissolved three months after the filing of the final papers with the CRO

 Key issues for consideration when deciding to wind up a company by a MVL

There are a variety of different matters that can impact on the planning and process of a members' voluntary liquidation. Outlined below is a non-exhaustive list of certain of the more common and important matters for consideration when contemplating or completing a members' voluntary liquidation.

Cash

A capital distribution received by a shareholder during the course of a liquidation is deemed to be a disposal of shares by the shareholder and is therefore subject to capital gains tax rates (as opposed to a distribution received by a shareholder other than in the course of winding up, which is deemed as income of the shareholder and is therefore liable to income tax).

A non-resident shareholder may not be subject to Irish Capital Gains tax on a distribution received from an Irish resident company, depending on how the shares in the company derived their value.

In the circumstances where a shareholder will require an early distribution of funds, the liquidator should ask the shareholder to sign an indemnity. An indemnity is an undertaking to effectively safeguard the liquidator against any unforeseen claims against the company.

In the absence of an indemnity the shareholder will receive a distribution of funds from the company when the liquidator is satisfied that all creditors have been paid and the affairs of the company are wound up.

Property

The disposal of property by a company in liquidation is a chargeable event for corporation tax which will give rise to a chargeable gain or loss. The company may be liable to capital gains tax on the chargeable gain.

The distribution in specie of a capital asset by a liquidator in respect of the shareholders shares is also deemed to be a disposal by the company for Capital Gains tax purposes.

The transfers of assets to the shareholders *in specie* in respect of their shares may qualify for exemption from stamp duty.

A charge to VAT may also arise on the disposal of a property. The company's advisors will be required to supply a VAT history for the property being disposed of and an opinion in relation to the charge of VAT thereon.

Under Section 41 of the Stamp Duty Consolidation Act a charge to *ad valorem* duty may arise on the distribution of a property *in specie* where a property is being transferred in satisfaction or partial satisfaction of a debt to a shareholder whether the debt is secured against the property or not.

Shares

All shares held by a company in liquidation can be transferred to a third party by way of distribution *in specie*.

The transfer of shares may give rise to a chargeable gain or loss thus the company may be liable to capital gains tax on the chargeable gain.

A disposal or transfer of the company's shares made after the date of liquidation can only be made with prior approval from the liquidator. Any disposal or transfer of shares or alteration in the status of the members of the company made after the commencement of a voluntary winding up, without the sanction of the liquidator, will be void.

Loans (Asset)

A loan that is written off over the course of liquidation may have tax implications for the company in liquidation depending on the type of transactions that compose the loans and advances figure. In particular, practitioners should be alert to historical items that were expensed through the Profit & Loss account or carried in an intercompany account.

The Company can also choose to assign the loan to another company by way of a distribution *in specie*.

Financial Services Companies

A company regulated by the Irish Financial Services Regulatory Authority (IFSRA) will need to revoke the authorisation of the company as a designated investment company.

The authorisation can be revoked provided final disbursement of assets to the participating shareholders has taken place; sufficient provision has been made for the costs of the liquidation and creditors per the termination accounts.

The liquidator may arrange for the revocation of the company's licence with the IFSRA.

The liquidator will then make a distribution of funds to the former shareholders of the fund.

Tax Returns

The date of liquidation will signal the end of an accounting period for tax purposes. The Revenue Commissioners will require that all tax returns are filed up to the date of liquidation and all related tax liabilities paid prior to the issue of a letter of tax clearance for the Company.

The company can reclaim VAT paid on liquidation expenses provided the company retains a vatable asset.

Charges

Any charge registered against the company's assets must be confirmed as satisfied prior to a distribution from the company. It may be necessary to file a Statutory Declaration of Satisfaction of a Charge (Form C6) or, in any event, obtain a letter from the charge holder confirming that they no longer rely on the charge registered against the company.

 Closing a members' voluntary liquidation

- confirm that all assets have been realised

- confirm that all liabilities are paid

- confirm that the affairs of the company have been fully wound up

- distribute any surplus funds to shareholders in accordance with their percentage shareholding and the priority of their shareholding

- complete the liquidator's final statement of account after payment of liquidation expenses and all known creditors and final distribution to the shareholders

- obtain confirmation from the Revenue Commissioners that all tax returns up to the date of liquidation are filed and paid

- de-register the company for taxes

- obtain clearance to hold the final meeting from all company advisors

- ensure that the books and records of the company will be held for a period of three years from the date of the final meeting in accordance with section 305 of the Companies Acts 1963– 2006

- reconcile and document the movement between the assets and liabilities noted on the declaration of solvency to the last set of audited accounts to ensure there are no material variations that have not been adequately explained

- advertise a notice of the final meeting in two daily newspapers circulated in the district of the registered office address of the company to include the time, place and the purpose of the meeting at least 28 days in advance of the final meeting

- issue a notice of the final meeting to members (usually in line with the timing of the advertisement)

- hold the final meeting, make a report to the meeting to show how the winding up has been conducted and the property of the company disposed of, and prepare minutes of the final meeting

- file the final CRO returns (**Form 13 and Form 14**) with the CRO within 7 days of the final meeting

- Confirm the dissolution of the company three months after filing the liquidator's statement of account

 **Case Studies**

Case Study 1 – *Property Company*

AIM

David Van Dessel was appointed liquidator to a company that held a property. The shareholders wanted to liquidate the company and transfer the property to a director.

RESULT

- The liquidator distributed the property *in specie* to the director.

- The property was deemed to be disposed by the company at market value.

- The gain on the disposal of the property gave rise to a capital gains tax liability for the company.

- The shares of the company were deemed to be disposed of by the shareholders. The shareholders were liable to capital gains tax on the disposal of their shares.

Case Study 2 – *Trading Company*

AIM

David Van Dessel was appointed liquidator to a software development company whose shareholder had decided to wind down operations in Ireland. The company, in addition to cash and debtor assets, held a lease on its premises and had employees at the date of liquidation.

RESULT

The liquidator arranged for the debtors to be collected and creditors to be paid in full. The liquidator liaised with the company's legal advisor on the surrender of the lease, and with the Department of Enterprise, Trade and Employment and the company's pension provider in relation to employee claims and pension options. All surplus funds were distributed to the shareholder.

The surplus cash distributed to the shareholder was treated as a capital distribution from the company. The shareholder was subject to capital gains tax liability on the funds received by the company.

Frequently Asked Questions

Q) Who is responsible for preparing the declaration of solvency?

A) The directors are responsible for preparing the declaration of solvency. It is the responsibility of the directors to ensure that the statement of assets and liabilities is true and accurate. In certain circumstances, the directors may be deemed personally liable for the obligations of the company.

Q) When is a declaration of solvency considered ineffective?

A) If the declaration of solvency is not made and delivered to the CRO in accordance with section 256 CA1963 as substituted by section 128 of the Companies Act 1990 (CA 1990).

If the declaration of solvency has a technical error; for example the name and

address of each director stated on the declaration of solvency must match the contact details held by the CRO for each director, otherwise the declaration will be returned. It may be necessary to file a **Form B10** (Notice of Change in Directors or Secretaries or in their Particulars) prior to filing the declaration of solvency.

Q) What are the consequences if a declaration of solvency is considered ineffective?

A) The resolution to wind up the company will remain valid and the winding up becomes a creditors' voluntary winding up. Section 266 CA 1963 then applies. The liquidator will be obliged to report to the new liquidator if so appointed or Office of the Director of Corporate Enforcement.

Q) What is required if a declaration of solvency is made outside the Irish jurisdiction?

A) A declaration of solvency sworn in a foreign jurisdiction that is party to the Hague Convention before a person entitled to administer oaths for that jurisdiction must be accompanied by a certificate of legalisation called an **apostle**. This confirms the capacity in which the person signing the document has acted and that the signature, seal or stamp of the person which the document bears, are certified. The apostle can be obtained from the designated authority for that jurisdiction.

A listing of countries that are party to the Hague Convention abolishing the Requirement of Legalisation for Foreign Public Documents can be obtained from the Hague Convention Website, **www.hcch.net**

No legalisation is required for a declaration of solvency sworn in countries that are party to the EC Convention abolishing the legalisation of documents in

Member States of the European Communities of 25 May 1987.

However, only Belgium, France, Denmark, Italy and Ireland are all party to the EC Convention.

Q) Do the directors retain their powers after the appointment of a liquidator?

A) All of the directors' powers cease, unless the members in general meeting or the liquidator gives permission to the directors to retain some of their power.

Q) Can a director sign documents on behalf of the company after the appointment of a liquidator?

A) The liquidator has sole signing authority on all documents signed on behalf of the company after the date of liquidation.

The directors may be asked to sign documents that relate to pre-liquidation periods, e.g. tax returns.

Q) Does the company have a statutory requirement to file Annual Returns when it is in liquidation?

A) No. The liquidator will file an annual account of his/her dealings and of the conduct of the winding up (**Form E3**).

Q) What happens if the company wants to reverse the Members' Voluntary Liquidation?

A) A company that is dissolved can be restored to its original status within two years of the dissolution (section 310 CA 1963).

The liquidator or any interested party will need to make an application to the High Court to have the resolution of winding up annulled. The liquidator, or the interested party, in their court application must justify their grounds for restoring the company

and demonstrate why restoration will be beneficial to the company. A simple change of mind, perhaps due to a change in circumstances or change in opinion on tax treatment may not be sufficient to convince the court of the benefits. Before the resolution is passed, the directors and shareholders should ensure that this is the appropriate course of action.

The person on whose application the order was made must file an official copy of the order with the CRO within 14 days after making the order, or within such further time as the court will allow.

If a company is still in liquidation, a liquidator or interested party on behalf of the company that is in liquidation, can petition a court to defer the date at which the dissolution of the company is to take effect for such time as the court thinks fit.

The person on whose application an order of the court is made must file an official copy of the order for registration with the CRO.

Q) Does the phrase "in voluntary liquidation" mean that all creditors will be paid in full?

A) In the context of a members' voluntary liquidation, all admitted creditors will be paid in full. However, the phrase *in voluntary liquidation* is also used to describe creditors' voluntary liquidations where, due to the company's insolvency, creditors are unlikely to be paid in full.

Q) How much are the liquidator's fees for a members' voluntary liquidation?

A) The fees for a members' voluntary liquidation depend on the extent of the work involved, is usually a fixed price agreed before the appointment and will generally be less than the fees charged for a creditors' voluntary liquidation.

Chapter >> **6**

Examinations and Schemes of Arrangement

Chapter 6 Overview

▶▶ What is an examination?

▶▶ What is an examiner?

▶▶ Legislation, and guidance from Chartered Accountants Ireland

▶▶ When is examination suitable/appropriate?

▶▶ Who are the key parties involved in an examination?

▶▶ Recent statistics and trends in examination

▶▶ Who can petition to place a company under the protection of the High Court and for the appointment of an examiner?

▶▶ Preparing a petition

▶▶ Preparing an independent accountant's report

▶▶ The effect of the appointment of the examiner

▶▶ Critical pre-petition liabilities

▶▶ Appointment of a creditors' committee

▶▶ Examiners' duties

▶▶ Contents of proposals for a scheme of arrangement

▶▶ The meetings of members and creditors

▶▶ The impairment of creditors' claims

▶▶ Examiner's report under section 18 C(A)A 1990

▶▶ Confirmation of proposals

▶▶ Timeline for an examination period

▶▶ Bringing an examination to a close and the cessation of Court protection

▶▶ Case Study – *ABC Ltd*

▶▶ Informal schemes of arrangement/other forms of rescue

▶▶ Case study – *Pye (Ireland) Limited*

▶▶ Conclusion

▶▶ Frequently Asked Questions

What is an examination?

Examination is a process whereby a company can be placed under the "protection" of the High Court from its creditors while its affairs are restructured.

Where a company is placed in examination, the examiner:

1] considers whether the company has a reasonable prospect of survival and is capable of rescue and, if so,

2] formulates a proposal for investment in the company and brings forward a scheme of arrangement for approval by the company's creditors and the High Court.

What is an examiner?

An examiner is an individual, usually an accountant, who is appointed to a company by the High Court and who assesses the affairs of the company that has been placed into examination and, if possible, prepares a plan for the rescue of the company, its undertakings or substantial parts thereof.

The examiner in this context should not be confused with the Office of the High Court Examiner as outlined in **Chapter 4.**

Qualifications of an examiner?

While it is usual that an examiner is a practising accountant, there is no requirement that examiners have any specific qualifications.

Certain parties are disqualified from being appointed as an examiner as follows:

- companies

- those who are connected with the company in question

- undischarged bankrupts

- persons who are the subject of a disqualification order are precluded from acting as examiner to a company

Also, a person cannot be appointed as examiner of a company if they are not eligible to be appointed as the company's liquidator.

Legislation, and guidance from Chartered Accountants Ireland

The main legislative provisions concerning examinations are set out in the following:

- Companies (Amendment) Act 1990 (C(A)A 1990)

- Part IX of the Companies Act 1990 (CA 1990)

- Part II of the Companies (Amendment) (No. 2) Act, 1999 (C(A)(No. 2)A 1999)

Guidance on best practice from Chartered Accountants Ireland

- SIP 19B – Appointment as Examiner under the Companies (Amendment) Act, 1990

This Statement of Insolvency Practice addresses:

- the statutory basis for appointment of an examiner

- the independent accountant's report

- timing, communication and administration in the examination process

- the role of the examiner; and powers and duties of directors of the company

 When is examination suitable/appropriate?

In general, an examination is suitable if the company:

- has a viable business

- has a reasonable prospect of survival after the examination has ended and

- a scheme of arrangement can be formulated for the approval by the company's members, creditors and the High Court.

The main factors that determine whether an examination is suitable for a company include:

- if the company has a trading business, but is likely to be presently insolvent

(i.e. cannot **currently** pay its debts as they fall due and/or the company's liabilities currently exceed its assets)

- if the circumstances that gave rise to the insolvency can be reversed, or were once off (i.e. a large bad debt)

- if the cashflow for the examination period is positive, i.e. the company will trade profitably during the examination period and will not worsen its financial position and that of its creditors

- if the company has investors who are willing to invest in the company

- if the company has a significant amount of trade creditors and/or tax liabilities

- if the company has the support of its secured bankers and has the ability to pay bank debts

- if the company has the cash to pay the petition costs

- if the company has the support of any critical creditors, whose refusal to support the examination would result in the collapse of the company

An examination is *not suitable* for a company when:

- the company is not trading

- the company has no cashflow

- the company does not have a realistic chance of obtaining an investor

- a period under the protection of the court is unlikely to address the reasons for the company's insolvency

- the affairs of the company are such that a restructing is not feasible

- the company has poor financial controls or management

- the company does not have support from its critical creditors

- the company's bankers / financiers are fundamentally opposed to the appointment of an examiner

- the company, if involved in construction, has a poor history of compliance with the Revenue Commissioners and is unlikely to obtain an up-to-date C2 Payments Card. (The failure to obtain a C2 payments card means that the company will have 35% deducted from payments received on contracts. This makes trading in examination significantly more difficult.)

The following, however, are circumstances where an application to appoint a examiner will certainly be refused:

- The High Court will not hear a petition to appoint an examiner under section 2 C(A)A 1990, which is presented by a creditor (be they confirmed creditors, contingent creditors or prospective creditors) until such security for costs has been given as the High Court deems reasonable, and until a prima facie case for the protection of the High Court has been established to its satisfaction.

- The High Court will not hear a petition under section 2 C(A)A 1990 if a receiver has been appointed over the

company for a continuous period of 72 hours prior to the presentation of the petition.

It should be noted that a refusal to grant the protection of the court can be appealed to the Supreme Court.

Who are the key parties involved in an examination?

The process of placing a company into examination is discussed in detail below. However, the main parties involved in the process are as follows:

- the company

- the petitioner(s)

- the independent accountant

- the High Court

- the examiner

- critical creditors, i.e. the Revenue Commissioners, employees, key suppliers

- other creditors and stakeholders

- shareholders

Recent statistics and trends in examination

As a result of the recent economic downturn, it can be seen that the number of examinations has increased considerably. During the course of the early to mid-2000s, the number of

Examinership Comparison 2007/2008/2009

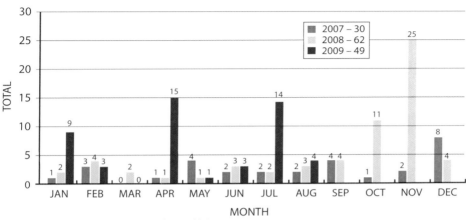

(Courtesy: www.insolvencyjournal.ie)

examination applications was consistently low. The upturn in examinations from 2007 onwards is very notable with an increase of 700% from 2006 to 2007 and the continuing rise in numbers in particular since the last quarter of 2008 (the figures for 2009 are to the end of August.)

Trends in examination

Other than the increase in the number of applications for the appointment of an examiner, there have also been very notable changes in the success rate and expectations surrounding examinations.

During the early to mid-2000s, the success rate for examinations was in excess of 90%. This clearly reflected not just the strong economic position in Ireland during this period, but was also indicative of accessibility to funds for potential investors.

2008 saw a substantial drop in the success rate of examinations to only 35%. Average distributions to the various classes of

creditors (dividends) from examinations also fell to 23% for preferential creditors and only 13% to unsecured creditors.

There have been a growing number of failing examinations during 2009, with some particularly high profile casualties. The failures demonstrate that there is a notable lack of cash fluid investors, a lack of bank funding and an increasingly downbeat view of business prospects given the current economic climate.

In light of the above, it is very notable that:

● Many companies are now failing to even achieve the protection of the High Court due to a lack of survival prospects.

● The High Court is assessing the assumptions on which the application (including the Independent Accountant's Report) for court protection is based with increasing scrutiny and scepticism.

Who can petition to place a company under the protection of the High Court and for the appointment of an examiner?

A petition under section 2 C(A)A 1990 to place the company in examination may be presented by:

1] the company, or

2] the directors of the company, or

3] a creditor, or contingent or prospective creditor (including an employee), of the company, or

4] members of the company holding at the date of the presentation of a petition under section 2 C(A)A 1990 not less than one-tenth of such of the paid-up capital of the company as carries at that date the right of voting at general meetings of the company, or

5] all or any of the above parties, together or separately

Note: It is important that the petition indicate if there is a need for the immediate appointment of an interim examiner pending the hearing of the full petition.

Preparing a petition

A petition presented under section 2 C(A)A 1990 must be accompanied by:

1] a letter of consent signed by the person nominated to be the examiner

2] the report of an independent accountant

3] if the proposals for a scheme of arrangement in relation to the company's affairs have been prepared for submission to interested parties for their approval, these should also be included with the petition

Preparing an independent accountant's report

Historically, the independent accountant's report has generally been prepared by the company's auditor, but can also be prepared by a qualified accountant or auditor who is independent of the company. Recent unfavourable High Court comments have resulted in an increasing move towards the completion of the report by an accountant wholly **unassociated** with the company. The independent accountant's report will include the following key sections:

● a cashflow projection for the examination period

● the pre-petition liabilities that the company has to pay

- the "conditions essential for the survival of the company"

- statement of affairs on a going concern basis

- statement of affairs on a winding up basis

- the names and addresses of the creditors of the company

 ## The effect of the appointment of the examiner

The company will be under the protection of the High Court from the day beginning with the presentation of the petition for the appointment of an examiner for a period of 70 days (or on the withdrawal or refusal of the petition, whichever happens first). The period of 70 days can be extended to 100 days on application by the examiner to the Court.

The Court may in certain circumstances appoint an interim examiner on the first day on which the company is under the protection of the court. The examiner is, however, not fully appointed until the hearing of the petition some days later. This effectively means that the company can be under the protection of the court, but that there is yet to be an examiner formally appointed.

For as long as a company is under the protection of the High Court, in a case under the Companies (Amendment) Act 1990, the following provisions will have effect:

1] no proceedings for the winding up of the company may be commenced, nor a resolution for winding-up be passed in relation to that company, and any such resolution passed will have no effect

2] a receiver cannot be appointed over **any part** of the property or undertaking of the company

3] no attachment, sequestration, distress or execution will be put into force against the property or effects of the company, except with the consent of the examiner

4] where any claim against the company is secured by a charge on the whole or any part of the property, effects or income of the company, no action may be taken to realise the whole or any part of such security, except with the consent of the examiner

5] no steps may be taken to repossess goods in the company's possession under any finance agreement, except with the consent of the examiner

6] no other proceedings in relation to the company may be commenced except by leave of the High Court and subject to such terms as the court may impose. The court may, on the application of the examiner, make such order as it thinks proper in relation to any existing proceedings, including an order to stay such proceedings.

7] complaints concerning the conduct of the affairs of the company while it is under the protection of the court will not constitute a basis for the making of an order for relief under section 205 CA 1963 (remedy for oppression of members of a company)

Critical pre-petition liabilities

Pre-petition liabilities are any liabilities owing to any creditor of the company before the protection of the Court is granted. Critical pre-petition liabilities are those outlined by the independent accountant's report and included in the petition to appoint the examiner, and which are considered to be essential for the survival of the company. These may include the payment of a liability to a key supplier without whose support and continued supply, the company will be unable to trade. The examiner, once appointed, can also seek approval from the High Court to discharge any additional pre-petition liabilities that he considers are essential for the survival of the company as a going concern during the protection period.

 ## Appointment of a creditors' committee

The independent accountant's report may recommend the appointment of a committee of inspection. An examiner may seek to have such a committee appointed. The High Court may also direct the appointment of a committee regardless of the views of the examiner or independent accountant.

Unless otherwise directed by the Court, a committee will not consist of more than five members and will include three of the largest unsecured creditors (who agree to be members of the committee). As with court liquidations, the appointment of a Committee of Inspection in an examination is rare.

 ## Examiners' duties

Examiners' duties regarding the formulation of proposals

- once an examiner is appointed, his main duty is to try to formulate rescue proposals for the company, which is known as a compromise of debt or a 'scheme of arrangement'

- the examiner is also obliged to carry out any other duties as ordered by the Court

- within 35 days of the appointment, the examiner is obliged to report to the High Court as to whether a scheme of arrangement can be formulated

- where the examiner is unable to formulate a scheme of arrangement, he will apply for the direction of the High Court, which will usually result in the winding up of the company

- if the examiner is able to formulate proposals for a scheme of arrangement for the rescue of the company, these proposals must:

  - specify the various classes of members and creditors, ensuring that the claims and/or interests of each particular class are treated equally, unless the holder of a particular claim agrees to less favourable treatment (in this regard, related parties often – but are not obliged to – agree to less favourable terms)

  - provide for the implementation of the scheme of arrangement

- specify any necessary changes to the management of the company or the Memorandum or Articles of Association of the company and include other matters as the examiner deems appropriate

- include a statement of the assets and liabilities of the company

- describe the estimated financial outcome of a winding up of the company for each class of members and creditors.

- the proposals are put to the meetings of each class of members and creditors. Along with the notice convening the meeting sent to the creditors and members, a statement must also be sent explaining the effect of the scheme of arrangement

- the proposals are deemed to have been accepted by a class of creditors when a majority in number and a majority in value of the claims represented at the meeting have voted in favour of the proposals

- The proposals are then brought before the High Court, which decides whether to accept or reject the respective proposals

The High Court cannot confirm the proposals unless:

- they have been accepted by at least one class of creditors in both number and in value whose interests would be impaired by their implementation,

- they are fair and equitable in relation to any class of members or creditors who have not accepted them and

whose interests would be impaired, and

- they are not unfairly prejudicial to any interested party. At the hearing, any member or creditor whose interests would be impaired by implementation of the proposals is entitled to object to their confirmation

If the High Court confirms the proposals, they are binding on all of the company's creditors included in the scheme of arrangement.

A guarantor's liability is not affected by the fact that the debt is the subject of a compromise or scheme of arrangement and parties who have given or have received personal guarantees should consult their legal advisors regarding the impact of an examination thereon.

Where the High Court makes modifications to the proposals, which alter them in a fundamental way, further meetings of the respective members and creditors need to be held.

In circumstances where the High Court refuses to accept the proposals, the company will lose the protection of the court and, in most circumstances, will be placed in liquidation or a receiver will be appointed, unless the refusal is subject to an appeal to the Supreme Court.

Examination of the affairs of company

As outlined previously, the appointed examiner has a duty to conduct an investigation into the affairs of the company. This investigation would not be as in depth as a report under section 56 of the CLEA 2001. However, the Court may order the review of any matter that it deems appropriate and the Examiner must be conscious of any matters of concern raised regarding the company.

Contents of proposals for a scheme of arrangement

Proposals for a compromise or scheme of arrangement must:

- specify each class of members and creditors of the company

- specify any class of members and creditors whose interests or claims will not be impaired or written down as part of the scheme of arrangement

- specify any class of members and creditors whose interests or claims will be impaired or written down by the proposals

- provide equal treatment for each claim or interest of a particular class unless the holder of a particular claim or interest agrees to less favourable treatment

- provide for the implementation of the proposals

- specify whatever changes should be made in relation to the management or direction of the company if the examiner considers that this is necessary to facilitate the survival of the company as a going concern

- specify any changes the examiner considers should be made in the Memorandum or Articles of the company

- specify any change in the management or direction of the company considered necessary

- any other matters that the examiner considers appropriate

- a statement of the assets and liabilities of the company as at the date of the proposals must be attached to each copy of the proposals to be submitted to meetings of members and creditors

- a statement of the assets and liabilities of the company prepared on a going concern basis must also be attached to each copy of the proposals to be submitted to meetings of members and creditors.

The meetings of members and creditors

The purpose of these meetings is to consider the proposals of the examiner as to the restructuring of the company's finances. This restructuring will almost certainly include some element of impairment of the claims against the company and the issue of impairment is dealt with in further detail below.

A minimum period of three days notice is required to be given in respect of the meetings of creditors and members. The meetings are held in a location convenient to the majority of members and creditors and a copy of the examiner's proposals are issued with the notice of the meeting.

The creditors are divided into different groups depending on the status and ranking of their claims against the company.

The shareholders are also divided into different groups depending on the ranking or type of their shares in the company (for example preferential shares and ordinary shares).

The meetings are chaired by the examiner and, once due consideration has been given to the proposals, a vote takes place. The proposals are deemed approved if a majority in number, which also represents a majority in value, of the claims against the company vote in favour of the proposals.

The impairment of creditors' claims

A creditor's claim against a company is impaired or written down if they receive less in payment of their respective claim than the full amount due at the date when the company was placed in examination.

The interest of a member of a company is impaired if:

- the nominal value of their shareholding in the company is reduced

- where they are entitled to a fixed dividend in respect of their shareholding in the company, the amount of that dividend is reduced

- they are deprived of all or any part of the rights accruing to him by virtue of their shareholding in the company

- their percentage interest in the total issued share capital of the company is reduced, or

- they are deprived of their shareholding in the company

Examiner's report under section 18 C(A)A 1990

Once the meetings of members and creditors are complete, the examiner prepares an examiner's report under section 18 C(A)A 1990, being effectively the proposals for the survival of the company placed in a report to be presented to the High Court.

The examiner will then deliver a copy of his report under this section 18 C(A)A 1990 to:

- the company on the same day as his delivery of the report to the High Court, and

- any interested party on written application

An examiner's report under section 18 should include:

- the proposals for the scheme of arrangement before the required members, and creditors, meetings

- any modification of the proposals at any of the meetings of members or meetings of creditors

- the outcome of each of the members' or creditors' meetings

- the recommendation of the committee of creditors (if appointed)

- a statement of the assets and liabilities of the company as at the date of the report

- a list of the creditors of the company, the amount owing to each such creditor, the nature and value of any security held by any such creditor, and the priority status of any such creditor under section 285 CA 1963 or any other statutory provision or rule of law

- a list of the officers of the company

- the examiner's recommendations for the company

- any other matters as the examiner deems appropriate or the High Court directs.

>> Confirmation of proposals

The report of the examiner under section 18 C(A)A 1990 should be set down for consideration by the High Court as soon as it is received.

The following persons may appear and be heard at a hearing:

- the company

- the examiner

- any creditor or member whose claim or interest would be impaired if the proposals were implemented.

At the hearing, the High Court may:

- confirm the proposals

- confirm subject to modifications, or

- refuse to confirm the proposals.

The court will *not* confirm any proposals:

- unless at least one class of members and one class of creditors whose interests or claims would be impaired by implementation of the proposals have accepted the proposals, or

- if the sole or primary purpose of the proposals is the avoidance of payment of tax due, or

- unless the High Court is satisfied that:

    1] the proposals are fair and equitable in relation to any class of members or creditors being impaired

    2] where the court confirms proposals (with or without modification), the proposals will be binding on all the members or class or classes of members, the creditors or class or classes of creditors as the case may be, affected by the proposal and also on the company.

The Court may also refuse to confirm the proposals if it forms the view that the company is not a vehicle suitable for survival as envisaged by the C(A)A 1990.

Any alterations in, additions to or deletions from the Memorandum and Articles of the company, which are specified in the proposals, will, after confirmation of the proposals by the High Court and notwithstanding any other provisions of the Companies Acts, take effect from a date fixed by the court.

Where the High Court confirms the proposals it may make such orders for the implementation of its decision as it deems fit.

A compromise or scheme of arrangement proposals that have been confirmed will come into effect on a date fixed by the court which cannot be later than 21 days from the date of their confirmation.

On the confirmation of the proposals, a copy of any order made by the High Court will be delivered by the examiner, or by such person as the court may direct, to the registrar of companies for registration.

However where:

- the High Court refuses to confirm proposals, or

- the report of an examiner under section 18 concludes that, following the required meetings of members and creditors of a company, it has not been possible to reach agreement on a compromise or scheme of arrangement,

the High Court may make an order for the winding-up of the company, or any other order as it deems fit.

Time line for an examination period

ex parte hearing/lodge petition papers (petitioner)	**Day 1**
Form E24 to be filed with CRO (petitioner)	**Day 3**
advertise in two daily newspapers (petitioner)	**Day 3**
confirmation hearing	**Day 10-12**
notice placed in *Iris Oifigiúil*	**Day 30**
interim report to High Court	**Day 35**
investment process	**Day 35-37**
request extension beyond 70-day period to • finalise scheme of arrangement and send to creditors • investment cash to be lodged to client account • hold meetings of members and creditors (at least three days after notices sent out) • S18 Report – to include summary of meetings/proposals	**Day 70**
final day • final High Court Order	**Day 100**

The dividend is usually paid within 30 days but this may be varied if approved as part of the scheme.

Bringing an examination to a close and the cessation of Court protection

The protection deemed to be granted to a company under section 5 C (A)A 1990 will cease on:

- the coming into effect of a compromise or scheme of arrangement, or

- on such earlier date as the High Court may direct.

- Where a company ceases to be under the protection of the High Court, the appointment of the examiner will terminate on the date of such cessation.

Case Study – *ABC Ltd*

BACKGROUND INFORMATION

- **Clothing retailer with turnover of €10 million**

- **Leases six premises in Dublin, paying "Boom level" market rents to landlords**

COMPANY BALANCE SHEET

a] Balance sheet prepared on "going concern basis"

● Assets:	€	€
Leasehold	1,600,000	
Stock		400,000
Fixtures & Fittings	1,500,000	
Goodwill	2,000,000	5,500,000
● Creditors:		
Revenue Commissioners	750,000	
Trade Creditors	1,500,000	
Bank Debt	1,000,000	
Leasing Obligations	1,000,000	
		4,250,000
Net Surplus/(Deficit)		**1,250,000**

b] Balance sheet prepared on "winding up/liquidation basis"

● **Assets:**	€	€
Leasehold	0	
Stock		100,000
Fixtures & Fittings	150,000	
Goodwill	0	250,000
● **Creditors:**		
Revenue Commissioners	750,000	
Trade Creditors	1,500,000	
Bank Debt	1,000,000	
Leasing Obligations	1,000,000	
Employee Entitlements	300,000	4,550,000
Net Surplus/(Deficit)		**4,300,000**

With the downturn in the economy, the company's turnover fell by 30% to 35% and the company expected turnover to remain at that level for two to three years. In particular, the turnover of a certain shop effectively collapsed.

The company was not in a position to pay all its outstanding debts and, after taking professional advice, it requested its auditors to prepare an Independent Accountant's report.

The independent accountant concluded that the company had a "reasonable prospect of survival" subject to the agreement of a scheme of arrangement with its creditors.

The company engaged its legal advisors to prepare petition papers to have the company placed in examination under the protection of the High Court.

Based on the petition papers and independent accountant's report, the High Court Judge made an order placing the company in examination.

As part of the restructuring, the company commenced negotiations with its landlords with a view to reaching agreement on reduced rents. The company succeeded in renegotiating reduced rent on several leases, on reduced rent in five premises, which were in non-prime shopping districts. The alternative of liquidation presented a worse alternative for the landlords involved.

However, one of the stores was loss-making to such an extent the company decided to close the store. The examiner made an application to repudiate the lease on this premises and ultimately included the landlord as a creditor in the scheme for an amount equal to the remaining duration of the lease. A specialist property advisor was engaged to quantify this amount and an agreement was reached with the landlord that he would be included in the scheme for a sum of €250,000. The company made twelve staff redundant in the process of closing this store. The Department of Enterprise, Trade and Employment (DETE) paid the employees redundancy entitlements directly to employees and the DETE ranked as a preferential creditor for that amount in the examiner's scheme of arrangement.

The examiner commenced drafting a scheme of arrangement between the company and its creditors and sought investors for the company.

Advertisements were placed in the national press, industry magazines, on relevant Internet sites (including www.insolvencyjournal.ie.)

The company in conjunction with the examiner approached its bank to seek re-negotiation of its repayment terms. The company reached an agreement to stretch out its repayments from two to five years and an interest roll-up on facilities for two years to allow the company some "breathing space" in the short term.

Many potential investors came forward and several offers were received.

Ultimately, an independent investor entered into an agreement with two of the four incumbent directors to invest a total of €750,000 in the company to cover the costs of the dividend payment to creditors, the costs of the examination and leave sufficient working capital in the company to finance future activities. This offer exceeded other offers and the examiner placed same in the proposals for consideration by the company's creditors.

The company signed an investment agreement with these investors with three conditions, being the approval of the examiner's scheme of arrangement by the shareholders, approval by the creditors and the subsequent approval of same by the High Court.

The examiner presented the scheme of arrangement below to a meeting of the members and each class of creditors. The members and all classes of creditors supported the scheme.

The examiner presented the scheme of arrangement including the voting results of the creditor meetings to the High Court. As at least one class of creditors had voted in favour of the scheme, the High Court approved the scheme and the dividends were paid to creditors within 30 days. Once the High Court order was given, the company formally exited the examinership process.

● Creditor	Debt	Dividend	Payment	*Debt Written Off
Preferential Creditors				
Revenue	750k	30%	225k	525k
Dept. Enterprise	100k	30%	30k	70k
Unsecured Creditors				
Trade Creditors	1,750k	20%	350k	1.4 million
Bank Debt	Company re-negotiates loan terms			
"Retention of Title" Creditors	Offered to collect goods remaining on site			
Leasing Creditors	Payments re-scheduled over 48 months			

Informal schemes of arrangement/other forms of rescue

Aside from the process of examination, there are certain other ways in which the affairs of a company can be restructured.

Informal Schemes of Arrangement

- an informal scheme of arrangement is a mechanism where a company or an individual agrees to pay a percentage of debts owing to creditors

- this informal arrangement does **not** involve the High Court and is significantly less costly

- there are a number of drawbacks associated with informal schemes of arrangement including:
  - any proposed dividend does not have to be accepted by a respective creditor
  - any creditor who does not wish to accept the proposal may institute legal proceedings

Other forms of rescue

Prior to the Companies (Amendment) Act 1990 and the inception of examination legislation, company law allowing for the negotiation, compromise or settlement of a company's debts with its creditors was provided for under sections 201 to section 204 of the CA 1963.

Section 201 CA 1963 provides that such a negotiation or compromise could occur when a company was in liquidation, where it was likely to be wound up, or where a restructuring of its share capital was proposed.

Section 201(1) prescribes that the proposed scheme or arrangement would be presented for approval to the members and creditors at a meeting(s) called by the High Court.

Section 201(1) also provides that the company, its members, any creditor, or the liquidator of a company may apply to the court for such a meeting to be held. This section provides for the formal initiation of the approval of a scheme of compromise between the company, its members and creditors.

Once an application is made under section 201(1), (2), the court has the power to restrain any proceedings against the company for any length of period that it saw fit. The process provides limited protection to the company. A receiver could be appointed over the company, although the company could have initiated this type of compromise process even after a receiver was appointed.

Section 201(3) describes the method as to how this type of compromise was to be approved by the members and the creditors of the company:

- each class of members and creditors had to be called upon to approve the scheme by a majority in number representing 75% of the value of those present at the respective meeting (this majority includes those voting by proxy)

- once approval had been obtained the company would then return to the

High Court for final approval. Once the scheme of arrangement was sanctioned by the High Court it was binding.

When a scheme of arrangement has been sanctioned by the High Court it must be publicised adequately. Section 201(5) provides that no order of the High Court sanctioning such a scheme would have effect until it was delivered to the CRO.

Case Study – *Re Pye (Ireland) Limited*

Potential problems with section 201 of the Companies Act 1963 were significantly highlighted in the case of *Re Pye (Ireland) Limited* (1984), where the litigation concerned the constitution of classes for the purpose of approving the scheme. The company owed money to secured, preferential and unsecured creditors. The Collector General was included in both the preferential and unsecured classes.

The classification of creditors became an issue when the Collector General was placed in the unsecured creditors in respect of its non-preferential debts along with another unsecured creditor who was also a 25% shareholder and who would benefit if the scheme was approved.

The High Court ruled that it would not sanction the scheme or arrangement where it considered that the classes of creditors had not been constituted correctly as the creditors had not been divided properly in accordance with interests.

This decision was appealed by the company to the Supreme Court in 1985.

The Supreme Court **held** that there was no need to constitute the classes separately on the grounds that the inclusion of the shareholder creditor did not mean that the classes had been improperly constituted unless it could be proved that the inclusion of certain interests in the class had prejudiced others in the class.

Section 279 scheme of arrangement

This is a similar process to a section 201 arrangement. However, this, in effect, can only be used when the company is being or is about to be wound up. There are considerable benefits to this form of a scheme as no court applications are involved and it is, therefore, a more cost-effective and less public form of arrangement.

Unfortunately, it is also burdened with the high level of approval to be obtained (both 75% of the number of creditors and 75% of the value of the claims). There is no court protection during the process and, ultimately, any creditor has a three-week window to bring an appeal of the terms of the scheme to the High Court.

Conclusion

The inherent flaws in the existing legislation as specifically demonstrated in the case of *Pye Ireland Limited* above coupled with the collapse of the Goodman empire led to the enactment of the examination legislation in 1990 and the examination legislation has proved to be very effective in recent years.

There are, however, significant restraints on the types of company which can successfully petition for court protection through the examination process. In particular, due to the cost of the process, examination is not a particularly viable option for SMEs (which represent the majority of Irish companies).

Frequently Asked Questions

Q) How long does an examination normally last?

A) An examination will last for an initial period of 70 days, which can be extended to 100 days by the examiner on application to the High Court if the examiner is of the opinion that the company has a reasonable chance of survival and there are investors willing to invest.

Q) What are the VAT implications for the company post-examination?

A) The claim of the Revenue Commissioners is crystallised at the date on which the petition for court protection is made. This is the claim included in the scheme of arrangement and no additional benefit/credit is given to Revenue for the fact that the company's trade creditors who, on being impaired, will seek to reclaim VAT from Revenue on the impaired portion of their debt.

Q) How does the company exiting examination account for VAT on credit notes received from its suppliers?

A) The fact is that it does not. Creditors should seek to recover the VAT from the Revenue Commissioners under bad debt relief and, therefore, do not issue credit notes to the company exiting examination.

Q) Can the company's auditor prepare the independent accountant's report?

A) Yes. Either the company's auditor or any independent auditor can prepare the independent accountant's report.

Q) Can a company's auditor act as examiner?

A) No. A company's auditor is deemed to be a connected party and hence is disqualified from being appointed as an examiner.

Q) What qualifications are required to be an examiner?

A) While it is usual that an examiner be a practising accountant, there is no requirement that they have any specific qualifications.

Q) Can the current promoters re-invest in the company?

A) Quite simply, yes, although this can give rise to tension with the company's creditors.

The investment process is, however, open to all interested parties and should be conducted with a view to maximising the return to creditors. This may easily include the sale of the business to parties unconnected to the company and the incumbent directors may lose control of the company as a result.

Q) What is meant by pre-petition liabilities?

A) Pre-petition liabilities are any liabilities owing to the creditors of the company before the protection of the court is granted.

Q) Does each class of creditor have to vote in favour of the examiner's scheme of arrangement for it to be sanctioned?

A) No, only one class of creditor whose claims are being impaired needs to vote in favour of the proposals for a scheme of arrangement for the scheme to be presented to the High Court for approval.

Q) When are the dividend payments made to the creditors?

A) The dividends to the creditors in a scheme of arrangement are usually paid within 30 days of the High Court approving the scheme of arrangement although this is subject to the terms of the scheme.

Q) What happens if the company does not secure investment?

A) If the company is unable to secure investment then the examiner will return to the High Court and seek the directions of the court as it is highly unlikely that a scheme of arrangement can be put in to place. It is likely that the company will therefore be wound up.

Q) What does "protection from its creditors" mean?

A) Protection from its creditors means that no proceedings can be taken against the company to enforce debts owing or repossess any assets encumbered or charged to a third party.

Q) Does the examiner take over the running of the company?

A) Unless specific executive powers are given to the examiner, the directors remain in the day-to-day control of the company's management.

Q) What powers does an examiner have?

A) An examiner has the power to:

- dispose of company assets

- access all company books and records

- convene, set the agenda for, preside at board meetings of the directors and general meetings of the company, and propose resolutions and present reports at such meetings

- repudiate a contract entered into by the company after his appointment if he considers it to be detrimental to the company

- apply to the High Court for the determination of any issue arising in the course of the examination

- apply to the High Court for the return of property disposed of by the company if he considers that the effect of the disposal was to perpetrate a fraud on the company or its creditors or members

- institute proceedings against directors or other persons including shadow directors for fraudulent or reckless trading seeking to make the person(s) involved personally responsible for all or part of the company's debts.

Q) Can an examiner be appointed if a receiver has already been appointed?

A) An examiner can only be appointed over a company within 72 hours of the appointment of a receiver. It is of particular note that this is a strict deadline and weekends and/or bank holidays have no bearing on this.

Q) Who is notified of the examiner's appointment?

A) The company and any notice parties and all connected stakeholders in the business are notified of the examiner's appointment.

Q) Are employee claims paid in an examination?

A) To the extent possible, ongoing wages should be discharged as normal while the company continues to trade.

In terms of pre-petition claims, the Department of Enterprise Trade and Employment (DETE) will pay out the statutory redundancy entitlements due to the former employees and will rank in the scheme of arrangement as a preferential creditor for 40% of the statutory amount paid out.

The DETE will not pay out any insolvency payments (minimum notice, arrears of wages and holiday) owing to the former employees. The statutory amounts owing to the employees in respect of insolvency payments must either be paid during the examination cash flow or ranked as a 100% creditor in the scheme of arrangement for the statutory amounts owing. The balance of any preferential or unsecured claims owing to the employees in respect of insolvency entitlement or expenses will also rank in the scheme for the respective dividend.

Q) How is the examiner paid?

A) The examiner's fees and expenses along with his legal fees and expenses will be paid from the assets of the company or the proposed investment in the company. If the examination fails and the company is placed in official liquidation or a receiver is appointed then the examiner's fees and expenses and his legal fees once approved by order of the High Court rank in priority to liquidator's or receiver's fees and expenses and preferential creditors and fixed and floating charge holders.

Q) What is the position of existing shareholders in an examination?

A) Usually, the existing shareholding is cancelled on agreement as they effectively have no value given the financial position of the company. It is of note that the High Court will not cancel shares without an agreement of the existing shareholders to do so.

Q) What is the success rate in examinations?

A) The success rate for examinations from 2000–2007 was in excess of 90%. However, the success rate for 2008 was circa 35%. This is primarily due to the lack of credit available for investors and tougher trading conditions due to the economic downturn.

Q) Is there a set dividend payout?

A) There is no set level for dividends. The average dividend payout in 2008 was 23% for preferential creditors and 13% for unsecured creditors. The main criteria for the level of distribution is that it should not be at a lower level than that which would be received if the company was wound up.

Q) Who generally invests in a company that is in examination?

A) Often the company's existing promoters, directors and senior management will invest in the company. Competitors too often use the opportunity to take control of a struggling competitor, expand and acquire greater market share. The company's largest customer/creditor may invest as the collapse of the examination may have severe repercussions on their trade or business.

Q) Will the examiner write down my company's bank borrowings to a level that the company will be able to service?

A) An examiner will review all options for the preparation of a viable scheme of arrangement and this may, in certain circumstances, include the write down of secured borrowings.

Q) What are the benefits of an examination for the creditors?

A) Creditors will receive a dividend in respect of their outstanding debt, which should be better than if the company were placed in liquidation or receivership where it is unlikely that they would receive any dividend (especially unsecured/trade creditors). Furthermore, the creditor will not lose a customer and there may be VAT and

corporation tax reliefs available on the write down of the debt.

Q) What are the disadvantages of an examination for the creditors?

A) The creditor may be forced to accept a dividend that is only a fraction of the debt outstanding and could result in potential insolvency for the respective creditor. In the event of the failure of an examination, the funds available for creditors are further, and usually substantially, reduced.

Q) What are the benefits of an examination for the company?

A) If the company has a large amount of historic debt then the scheme of arrangement will allow the company to effectively write off its liabilities for a fraction of the sum due.

Q) What are the disadvantages of an examination for the company?

A) The placing of a company into examination may result in certain creditors refusing to continue to trade with the company, clients refusing to discharge their debts or to do business in the future due to a perceived uncertainty about the company.

Q) How does the company deal with the Revenue Commissioners in an examination?

A) Once the Revenue Commissioners confirm both their preferential and unsecured claims against the company as at the date the examination commences, these will be placed in the scheme of arrangement. The company's tax liabilities arising during the examination must be discharged in full when the respective liabilities fall due. Failure to do so may result in the High Court taking an adverse view of the company's prospects.

Q) Do vital pre-petition liabilities approved by the High Court have to be discharged or can they be placed in the scheme?

A) Generally pre-petition liabilities that have been approved for payment by the High Court are deemed to be essential for the survival of the company. However, if it transpires that any respective approved pre-petition liability is not essential for the survival of the company then it does not have to be discharged and can be placed in the scheme of arrangement.

Q) How much does an examination cost?

A) The pre-petition costs to appoint an examiner usually amount to between €30,000 and €40,000 to include legal and independent accountant's costs.

However, it is very difficult to definitively state the level of the costs of the

examination as this is dependent on many matters such as the number of creditors, shareholders, the level of interest from potential investors, the complexity of the case and the number of applications to the Court that may be required.

However, it is possible to estimate that, in a relatively straightforward examination, the examiner's fees for the examination period are usually between €50,000–€100,000 and legal fees for the examination period are usually of the order of €30,000–€50,000.

If a company is suitable for examination, there are investors willing to invest and, subject to the approval of the company's creditors and the High Court, an examination can be a very cost-effective method of reducing a company's historic liabilities.

Example

Preferential Creditors			€1 million
Unsecured Creditors			€3 million
Total Liabilities			**€4 million**
Investment	€1.1 million		
Preferential Dividend	38.5c:€1	€385,000	
Unsecured Dividend	20c:€1	€600,000	
Examiner's Fees		€75,000	
Legal Fees		€40,000	**€1.1 million**
Write down Liabilities	€4.0 million		
Cost of Examination	(€1.1 million)		**€2.9 million**

Chapter >> 7

Investigations

Chapter 7 Overview

>> What is an investigation?

>> Liquidators' duties to the Office of the Director of
Corporate Enforcement (ODCE)

>> Restriction applications (pursuant to section 150 CA 1990)

>> Disqualification applications (pursuant to section 160 CA 1990)

>> Fraudulent and reckless trading

>> Fraudulent preference

What is an investigation?

An investigation is a review of the affairs of a company to determine if there are any rights of action as regards the directors of the company or any other party.

There are certain statutory duties required of liquidators and examiners to review the affairs of any company in this regard. While a receiver may not have the same statutory duty, a receiver also has the right to take legal proceedings on behalf of the company, be it against the directors or some other party.

The purpose of an investigation is to:

- determine the assets and liabilities of the company,

- determine the reasons for the failure of the company, and

- review the conduct, decisions and actions of the directors.

If, during the course of the investigation, any apparent preferences or rights of action come to light, the liquidator should determine, if necessary with the benefit of legal advice, whether or not any particular transactions can/should be set aside.

The extent and nature of any investigation work will vary from company to company but will invariably include the following:

1. Question Management

The liquidator will determine which directors (officials, former directors, de facto directors or shadow directors) held office during the last two years. These directors will be questioned as to the company affairs, specifically their understanding of the reasons for the failure of the company and their role and responsibilities within the company.

There are two particular phrases of note that are often incorrectly put forward regarding individuals' roles and responsibilities within a company, and these are as follows:

A **de facto director** is a person who has acted in the role of director and held themselves out to be a director, though they have not been formally appointed as such.

A **shadow director** is someone who ultimately controls the company and to whom the listed directors report, though this shadow director has not been formally appointed as a director.

The importance of properly identifying de facto directors and shadow directors is that such directors are also included in the liquidator's report to the Director of Corporate Enforcement pursuant to section 56 of the Company Law Enforcement Act 2001 (CLEA 2001).

2. Committee of Inspection (if appointed)

The liquidator will invite members of the committee of inspection to bring to his or her attention any particular matter they feel requires further investigation.

3. Examination of minute books and other records

The liquidator will seek to verify any statements made by directors in response to the questioning of management, by reviewing company files and papers in their possession. They will also seek to establish whether any significant business or any other transaction exceeded the powers of the directors.

4. Comparison of assets with last audited accounts

For the purposes of identifying assets, the **statement of affairs** is compared with the last audited accounts. The liquidator will wish to be satisfied that material movements in fixed and current assets can be properly explained. Sales of non-current assets over the preceding two years are examined to ensure that market value was obtained for them.

5. Trading Losses

The liquidator will seek to verify the level of trading losses and understand the reasons for same.

6. Transactions with related companies and connected persons

The books and records of the company are examined to ensure that any transactions with related companies or connected persons were carried out at arm's length. Particular attention will be paid to:

- transactions involving directors, including loans given by the company,

- any reduction in loan accounts and/or reduction in overdrafts and

- other debts supported by personal guarantees.

7. Unearth any rights of action of the liquidator

The liquidator's investigation into the affairs of the company aims to unearth any rights of action which the company or the liquidator may have against third parties

8. The liquidator considers whether the company traded fraudulently or recklessly

In considering fraudulent and reckless trading the liquidator seeks to determine:

- the reasons for the failure of the company

- the date when one or more of the directors became aware of the company's insolvency, or should have been aware

- the steps taken by the directors to address the company's difficulties

- the reasons for continuing to trade after the time they knew, or ought to have known, of the company's insolvency

- when a reasonable business person would have ceased to trade

The liquidator will then use the information gathered and report to the Director of Corporate Enforcement on their findings.

Liquidators' duties to the Office of the Director of Corporate Enforcement (ODCE)

As mentioned in **Chapter 2**, liquidators of insolvent companies have a statutory obligation to report to the ODCE pursuant to section 56 CLEA 2001 within six months of the date of their appointment. Section 56 CLEA 2001 amends section 150 of the Companies Act 1990 (CA 1990) by introducing an obligation on liquidators of insolvent companies to bring a restriction application against the directors of the company, unless relieved from this obligation by the Director of Corporate Enforcement.

Section 56 CLEA 2001 therefore places an obligation on liquidators to investigate the affairs of an insolvent company and in particular to comment on the following areas:

1. The reasons for the liquidation of the business

To **determine the reasons for the liquidation**, the liquidator would undertake the following:

- a review of the fall in the company's net asset position, including a review of the last audited financial statements to the statement of affairs

- a review of the company's trading losses and the reasons for these

- an analysis of the chairperson's statement

- a review of the minutes of the meeting of creditors

- discussions with creditors, the committee of inspection and the Revenue Commissioners

- identify prior insolvency appointments

- discussions with the directors

2. The extent of any deficiency in the payment and filing of taxes

To properly ascertain the extent of the company's compliance with the payment and filing of its taxes, a liquidator will implement the following:

- complete a schedule of unpaid and unfiled taxation returns

- obtain the details for preparation of the company's outstanding taxation returns

- verify the returns filed agree to the company's records by running sales and purchases, VAT reports and PAYE/PRSI reports

- examine the bank accounts for any untaxed payments to employees

- obtain details of any previous audits completed by the Revenue Commissioners

3. The identity of the controlling interest in/directors of the company

To determine the controlling interest, the liquidator would undertake the following:

- Question the known management and directors

- Seek the input of the Committee of Inspection

- Review the company's minute book
- Discuss the company with the pre-liquidation legal and financial advisors to the company
- Obtain copy ID and utility bills from the directors
- Review the auditors' comments regarding controlling interests and shareholdings in the audited financial statements

4. The honesty of the company's directors

To examine the directors' honesty, a liquidator will carry out the following:

- review of the chairperson's statement to and answers at the meeting of creditors, as opposed to the information gleaned from the company's records
- review the extent to which the company appears to have continued to trade while in financial difficulty solely to benefit the directors or related parties
- review of the company's bank account, cash receipts and payments
- review of trading with related parties/loans/personal guarantees
- review of the company's credit cards
- a review of the under declaration of taxes or switching names or utilising another party's C2 for the purpose of avoiding relevant contracts tax declaration
- a review of the company's invoicing to identify any false invoicing (invoice discounting)
- a review of the sales ledger vs outstanding debtors
- review of stock system vs available stocks
- review of fixed asset ledger vs available assets
- seek the input of the committee of inspection

5. The responsibility of the company's directors

While there is likely to be a significant overlap with the review undertaken to confirm the honesty of the directors, to examine the responsibility of the directors' actions a liquidator will review the following:

- the trading losses
- taxation compliance (filing and payment)
- the company's compliance with company law
- the maintenance of the company's books and records
- co-operation with the office holder/liquidator
- pension payment compliance/employee entitlements
- insurance compliance (employers and indemnity)

6. The identity of any related companies and review of related trading

The purpose of this review is to identify related parties that may have unduly benefited from the collapse of or from trading with the company. To this end, a liquidator will carry out:

- a review of trading/bank transactions with related parties

- a review of any new or recently commenced trading by related companies in the same industry (the 'Phoenix' syndrome)

- a review of previous directorships, restrictions or disqualifications

The liquidator will also seek the input of the committee of inspection, auditors and legal advisors.

7. The accuracy of the statement of affairs

To determine the accuracy of the statement of affairs, the liquidator should carry out an examination of the company's affairs to determine:

- assets not identified or values overstated

- liabilities understated

- is the deficit so large that the directors knew that it could not be recovered?

- fraudulent preference (the payment of a creditor with undue preference)

- misappropriation/fraud

- phoenix syndrome (whereby a new company improperly rises from the ashes of an insolvent predecessor)

- grounds for a restriction application pursuant to section 150 CA 1990

- grounds for reckless trading

8. Material transfers of assets

The key areas for a liquidator to review under this heading are as follows:

- 'Phoenix Syndrome'

- transfer of leased assets

- reviews for fraudulent preference

- review of stock system vs available stocks

- review of fixed asset ledger vs available assets

9. The date of the company's insolvency

It can be very difficult to definitively state a date for a company's insolvency. However, there are many matters that can point to the date of insolvency:

- the age profiles of the outstanding liabilities to creditors

- the extent of judgments and/or litigation against the company

- the age profile of arrears to the Revenue Commissioners, often coupled with a failure to submit tax returns

- the age profile of arrears to pension companies

- return dates for statutory returns being missed

- the transfer of business and/or assets

- the incorporation of a company to "take over" the business of the company moving towards liquidation

- minutes of meetings/internal memoranda

- management accounts

10. Any litigation against the company

For this purpose the liquidator should contact the company's pre-liquidation legal advisors and complete a judgment search in the Companies Registration Office to determine:

- proceedings ongoing against the company

- judgments registered against the company

The above reviews should be completed in accordance with the following Statements of Insolvency Practice from Chartered Accountants Ireland:

- SIP S2A – A liquidator's Investigations into the Affairs of an Insolvent Company – Northern Ireland

- SIP 2B – A liquidator's investigation into the affairs of an insolvent company

as well as the findings in the cases of *Re Squash (Ireland) Limited* and *Re La Moselle Clothing Limited* (which are discussed later in this chapter).

Restriction applications (pursuant to section 150 CA 1990)

Section 150 CA 1990 provides that, where restriction proceedings have been issued against a director, unless the director can demonstrate to the court that he acted honestly and responsibly in relation to the conduct of the affairs of the company **AND** that there is no other reason why it would be just and equitable that he should be restricted, the court will impose a restriction on the director. The provision contains an exception for directors who have been appointed by either a financial institution or a venture capital company. However, these exceptions are subject to the provision requiring a director to show that he acted honestly and responsibly.

As mentioned earlier in this chapter, the liquidator should report to the ODCE within six months of his appointment. In general, after three to four months from the receipt of the report from the liquidator, the ODCE will let the liquidator know whether restriction proceedings are required against the directors of the company. If the liquidator is required to make a restriction application, they must have **issued** the proceedings no later than five months after the date when the section 56 liquidator's report was submitted to the ODCE.

In the case of *La Moselle Clothing Limited* (1998), Mr Justice Shanley described the primary purpose of section 150 as being

> "the protection of the public from persons who, by their conduct, have shown themselves unfit to hold the office of a director and as a result represent a danger to potential

investors and traders dealing with such companies".

In forming judgment in this matter, Mr Justice Shanley outlined **five tests** that have proven to be the basis on which the responsibility of a director should be determined:

1] the extent to which the director has or has not complied with any obligation imposed on him by the Companies Acts 1963–1990

2] the extent to which his conduct could be regarded as so incompetent as to amount to irresponsibility

3] the extent of the director's responsibility for the insolvency of the company

4] the extent of the director's responsibility for the net deficiency in the assets of the company disclosed at the date of winding up or thereafter

5] the extent to which the director, in his conduct of the affairs of the company, has displayed a lack of commercial probity or want of proper standards

These tests were subsequently approved by Mrs Justice McGuinness in giving the views of the Supreme Court in *Re Squash (Ireland) Limited (2001)*.

Exceptions

Once the proceedings are issued against a director, the onus is on the director seeking to avoid restriction to prove that he acted honestly and responsibly, or that he falls within one of the exceptions contained in subsection 150 (2). The exceptions are:

"a] that the person has acted honestly and responsibly in relation to the conduct of the affairs of the Company and that there is no other reason why it would be just and equitable that he should be subject to the restrictions imposed by this section, or

b] subject to paragraph (a) that the person concerned was a director of the company solely by reason of his nomination as such by a financial institution in connection with the giving of credit facilities to the company or

c] subject to paragraph (a), that the person concerned was a director of the company solely by reason of his nomination as such, by a venture capital company in connection with the purchase of or subscription for, shares by it in the company."

Implications for a restricted director

In broad terms, the main implications for the restricted director are as follows:

● He will be restricted from acting as a director of a company for five years, unless that company meets conditions set out in section 150(3), which are that the nominal value of the allotted share capital of the company is as follows and fully paid up:

 ● €317,435 in the case of a PLC

 ● €63,487 in the case of any other company.

● If a restricted director acts in breach of section 150, he may be personally liable for the debts of the subsequent company if it goes into insolvent liquidation if the restriction provisions were not properly observed. Criminal sanctions may also apply.

- A person who has been restricted under section 150 can, within 12 months of making the order, apply to the High Court for relief, in whole or in part, against the restrictions under section 152 CA 1990.

- Notice of the restriction is placed on an easily accessible list available on the Website of the Companies Registration Office, **www.cro.ie**

Disqualification applications (pursuant to section 160 CA 1990)

In addition to the provisions of section 150, section 160(1) CA 1990 allows, on application to the High Court, for the disqualification of any person from acting as a director, auditor, other officer, receiver, liquidator or examiner, or be concerned in any way, directly or indirectly in the promotion, formation or management of any company.

Section 160(2) gives the court discretion to disqualify a person in a number of circumstances, generally involving conduct of a more serious nature than that required in order for a restriction order to be made.

Section 160 applies where a person is convicted of an indictable offence in relation to a company or involving fraud or dishonesty. The ODCE has used the provisions of this Act extensively in its investigations.

There are other specific incidences which may trigger an application for a disqualification order. These essentially involve allegations of serious wrong-doing by a director that would render him unfit to be involved in the management of a company. Directors can choose whether or not to defend the disqualification application.

The court has discretion about the period of disqualification when making a section 160 order. However, given the more serious nature of the offences in question, it is likely that the period involved will be longer than the mandatory five-year restriction under section 150. If a court decides to disqualify a director, it will then have to consider the appropriate duration of the disqualification and submissions will be heard from legal counsel for both the directors and the liquidator.

Fraudulent and reckless trading

A liquidator may institute proceedings against directors or other persons, including shadow directors, for fraudulent or reckless trading, seeking to make such persons personally responsible for all or part of the company's debts.

Criminal liability can also be imposed on a person found guilty of fraudulent trading. An officer of the company, such as a director or secretary, can be held personally liable where it appears that, while he or she was an officer, he or she was knowingly a party to the carrying on of the business of the company in a reckless manner.

Furthermore, any person, whether an officer or not, can be made personally liable if he or she was knowingly a party to the carrying on of any business of the company with intent to defraud its creditors or for any fraudulent purpose.

An officer is deemed to be knowingly a party to reckless trading where he or she was party to the carrying on of the business and ought to have known that his or her actions, or those of the company, would cause loss to the creditors.

An officer is also deemed to be knowingly a party to reckless trading where he or she was party to the contracting of a debt by the company and did not honestly believe on reasonable grounds that the company would be able to pay the debt when it fell due for payment as well as its other debts.

The High Court has the power to relieve any person of liability, in whole or in part, where it appears that the person concerned acted honestly and responsibly in relation to the affairs of the company.

 Fraudulent preference

The structure of Irish insolvency is based on the **equitable treatment of creditors** and the **payment** of same in terms of a **strict legal preference** as follows:

» **Fixed Charge/Mortgage holders**
  Usually the Company's bankers who have taken security over an asset

» **Super Preferential Claim**
  A claim of the Revenue

Commissioners in respect of unpaid employee PRSI

» **Preferential Creditors:**
  • unpaid taxes (usually) arising in the last 12 months

  • employee claims (including those of directors) subject to certain limits

  • commercial rates (usually) arising in the last 12 months

» **Floating Charge**
  • usually the company's bankers who have taken security over an asset

» **Unsecured Creditors**
  Despite the legal preference, when faced with insolvency, it is often the case that a director may

  • repay an overdraft, loan or supplier account on which he has given a personal guarantee

  • "sort out" a supplier with whom he has a long standing relationship

  • ensure that the company continues to pay rent on premises rented from related parties for as long as possible.

Section 286 CA 1963 enables an insolvency practitioner to invalidate a payment to any creditor outside of the terms of their ranking. In order to do so, each of the following basic matters must be proved by the practitioner:

• that there has been a transfer of a company asset or assets

• that this transfer has given a creditor a preference over similarly ranking creditors

- that the company was unable to pay its debts as they fell due at the time of the transfer, and
- that the transfer occurred within six months of the winding up of the company

The onus of proof is on the liquidator to demonstrate a dominant intention to prefer (i.e. that the transaction was completed for the purpose of giving a party a higher standing than entitled). However, in the case of a transfer to a connected party (as outlined in section 286(5) CA 1990) there **is a presumption** that the transaction took place with a view to preferring the connected party. Furthermore, in the case of a transaction to a related party, the transfer can be reversed if it occurred within two years of the winding up of the company (as opposed to six months in the case of an unconnected party).

Section 139 CA 1990 further strengthens the powers under section 286 CA1963 in that a creditor or contributory can also have a transaction set aside if the Court deems that the effect of the transaction was to perpetrate a fraud on the company, its creditors or its contributories.

The ultimate impact of the reversal of any such transaction is that the director would still have to pay any personal guarantee. However, this may be coupled with substantial legal costs.

Conclusion

The above represents the more regularly occurring rights of action of insolvency practitioners in their investigation of a company's affairs. These, however, represent only a small portion of the overall legislation and, therefore, in any circumstances where a practitioner, company advisor or director believe that breaches of company/criminal law have or may have occurred, it is important to source independent legal advice. (For this reason, and unlike in other chapters in this book, the Frequently Asked Questions section is not included here.)

Chapter >> *8*

Advising a Client in Financial Difficulty:

Consensual Restructuring and Enforced Solutions

Chapter 8 Overview

Introduction

In this chapter we will:

- introduce you to what we refer to as 'The Business Decline Curve', and the various stages of decline typically faced by a company in financial difficulty,

- introduce the possible solutions applicable at each of those stages, and

- highlight typical problems encountered with the implementation of those solutions.

Note: The focus here is on **limited liability companies**, rather than sole trader or partnership entities, and the solutions put forward only apply to limited liability companies.

At the time of writing, the global economy is suffering from a major economic depression; many financial institutions are in danger of crumbling under the weight of toxic debt; and many governments across the globe have been forced to step in with national funds to prevent the total collapse of their financial systems.

'Recession', 'downturn' and 'credit crunch' are the common parlance of the day, and the effects of the credit crunch have spread from the banking sector and have firmly taken hold in Ireland's business community.

In Ireland, like many Western European economies, the small and medium enterprises, (SME) sector is a major element of our economy and this chapter will focus on such SME companies as the typical profile of the client in financial difficulty. It is in this SME sector that business decline, once commenced, is most rapid and the need for immediate action is most critical.

 # The 'Business Decline Curve'

The Business Decline Curve

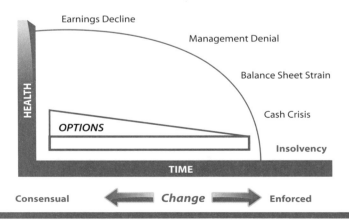

Courtesy of Begbies Traynor

The Business Decline Curve shows the slide of a company towards insolvency.

The message from the business decline curve is that the number of options available to a company in financial difficulty, and the appeal of those options, diminish as management delay their reaction to the warning signs.

Early and decisive action is the cornerstone of an effective survival plan. In the absence of such action, the company will rapidly find itself sliding down the business decline curve towards insolvent liquidation.

While management inaction continues, the options available to the struggling company move from consensual to enforced, as creditors begin to lose patience with, and trust in, the management team. The solicitors' letters begin to accumulate and it is only a matter of time (usually a significantly shorter period of time than that optimistically anticipated by the management team)

before a 21-day notice of petition to wind up arrives. By this point, the company is probably beyond recovery and is more than likely facing insolvent liquidation.

The importance of reliable financial reporting systems

However, when the management have financial reporting systems in place that produce the type of information required to manage a company, and when the management team have the expertise and/or the business acumen to understand that information, then the management team will be in a position to recognise the early warning signs.

Being able to recognise the early warning signs will enable the management team to react early and, importantly, gives them access to the more consensual corporate recovery solutions, as opposed to the outcome of enforced liquidation.

The Solutions

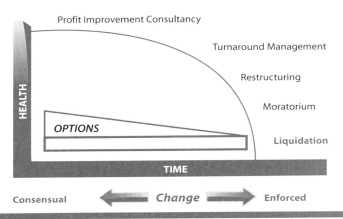

Courtesy of Begbies Traynor

A well-run financial reporting system is an absolute necessity for the proper management of any company. For companies in difficulty, having adequate financial reporting systems enables management to react to financial problems at the top of the business decline curve. **Earnings decline** is a typical warning sign (for the sake of clarity, earnings decline in this context refers to a decline in profit rather than a decline in turnover).

As insolvency practitioners, we are often surprised at the number of companies that are managed without the benefit of monthly or even quarterly management accounts. It is not uncommon for a director to tell us that they manage their business by knowing the approximate level of their liabilities to creditors and how much they have in the bank. This type of financial management is simply inadequate and directors who operate their business with such rudimentary methods often realise the true depth of their financial problems too late to react in any meaningful way. As a result, it is such companies that seek professional assistance when it is too late for the professional to provide a solution and, unfortunately, insolvent liquidation is too often the only realistic option.

Accountants are uniquely placed to educate clients on the importance of having a reliable financial reporting system. However, we must appreciate that not all SMEs are of a size and capability that they can properly manage an adequate financial reporting system in-house. In such circumstances, the directors of such SMEs must consider outsourcing their financial reporting system.

At a minimum, the company should maintain basic day books, such as purchases, sales, cash receipts and cheque payments, and these books should be updated on a regular basis. Those day books should then be forwarded on a monthly, or perhaps quarterly basis, to their external accountant for the production of management accounts.

The frequency will be determined by the size of the company and the quantum of transactions in any one period of time. However, we would suggest that at a minimum quarterly management accounts are necessary to enable directors to effectively manage a company. Failure by directors to maintain proper financial management might be viewed by the regulatory authorities, such as the Office of the Director of Corporate Enforcement (ODCE), as a failure in the carrying out of their duties and responsibilities as directors, with associated criminal and civil penalties.

Historically, the relationship between external accountant and the SME corporate client has revolved around the statutory audit. We believe that the annual statutory audit has sometimes promoted a behaviour in directors (in the SME sector) to produce reliable financial information only on an annual basis and has not sufficiently emphasised the importance of reliable management accounts throughout a financial year. Attempts to lift the audit burden on SMEs by raising the thresholds on which audits are based may amplify this behaviour. However, it is generally hoped that the tendency to view accounts as an annual task will change in the Irish SME sector, as companies give more priority to good corporate governance, responding to the work of organisations such as the ODCE in communicating its importance.

⏩ The human factor

As we are all aware, proper systems in themselves are only part of the solution; we must account for the human factor. Although an entity might have a reliable financial reporting system, which gives the right information, its management team need not only recognise the early warning signs, but also react to them.

Management denial is particularly acute where manager, director and shareholder are rolled into one person or a small number of connected persons (the typical, family-run private limited company). In Ireland, our important SME sector is most commonly comprised of companies with this profile, so it is fair to say that management denial is a very common problem in Irish business.

Management denial derives from the fact that the people in charge have so much to lose if the business actually fails, that their judgement can be clouded. This clouded judgement is often exacerbated by the fact that many SME companies, particularly the poorly-managed ones, are overly-focused on turnover rather than profit, leading management to look for more sales, and more contracts to overcome their problems, rather than focusing in on the true source of the problem, which often lies in their **basic cost structure**.

So, even where a company has a proper financial reporting system, which produces the early warning signs, an inappropriate reaction from management can force the company further down the business decline curve.

Reliable information and effective management

What is needed is a decisive and professional management team that is able to read the early warning signs and is willing to react in an effective and focused manner to steer the company away from enforced change.

The particular solutions implemented will be unique to each company's problems, and we do not intend to discuss them in detail here. Suffice it to say, that an effective management team will know the intricacies of their business and will, with early action, have time to prepare and implement an appropriate recovery plan.

"The Buy-in": acceptance of the need for and the process of addressing business decline

Before discussing the strategy to tackle the problem of business decline, there are a number of pre-requisites for a successful corporate recovery project, which advisors should be satisfied are in place before the commencement of the project. Such pre-requisites include:

- a willingness on the part of directors to take advice and to make hard decisions

- the ability to take early corrective action to maintain the support of both customers and creditors

If the directors are not willing to take the advice or are unwilling to make the necessary tough decisions, the corporate recovery project will not work.

As well as 'buy-in' from the directors and the management team, of equal importance is buy-in from the customers and creditors. In our experience, where the directors have shown their commitment to the corporate recovery project and where they have acted in good time, it is unusual for the customers and the creditors not to also buy in.

The key factor for the customers and the creditors is early action on the part of the directors. It is probable that the customers and the creditors, although they may be somewhat unhappy that they are caught up with a corporate recovery project, will see the commercial realities of the situation and will be willing to work with the company in order to avoid the more negative situation of a full-blown insolvency, which would likely have a negative impact for both the customers and the creditors. In an insolvency situation, the customers lose continuity of supply and have the disruption of selecting a new supplier, while creditors have both disruption to their business, caused by the loss of a customer, as well as the associated financial loss to endure.

Initial steps in formulating a restructuring plan

Before beginning to formulate a restructuring plan, it is important to remember that a restructuring comprises more than just a financial restructuring project: it should combine both financial and operational factors.

The ultimate objective of the restructuring project is to integrate financial and operational restructuring to re-build the business into a sustainable and lasting organisation. Therefore, a corporate restructuring professional is more than just a financial person. He or she must have the ability to operate outside of the financial world, and work with the directors in their particular, industry-specific areas of expertise.

Operational restructuring is far-reaching and is specific to particular projects, but would typically include such matters as:

● management change,

● re-alignment of strategic goals,

● review of supply chain management,

● review of costings and/or

● a review of processes.

The objective of operational restructuring is to create cost efficiencies in order to create a sustainable and lasting organisation.

Financial restructuring, on the other hand, involves how the business is financed, and typically relates to how arrears of debt are going to be renegotiated and then discharged over time, while keeping current liabilities up-to-date.

Financial restructuring tools include:

● conversion of debt to equity,

● issuing preference shares,

● issuing new classes of debt instruments,

● renegotiating covenants, and

● assessing the relationship between asset values and related security instruments.

A financial restructuring is not enough on its own: there must be a root and branch review of the business, and operational change must follow that review.

Formulating a restructuring plan

Restructuring plans require a focused approach and are best delivered in a short time-frame. Plans are often formulated under crisis conditions and are complex documents, which evaluate:

- the management team in place,

- the current business model, and

- the company's overall viability.

As mentioned before, restructuring plans must encompass both the financial and operational aspects of the business.

In essence there are **five key stages** or elements to restructuring plans:

1| **Analyse**

2| **Stabilise**

3| **Advocate**

4| **Re-organise**

5| **Improve**

1. Analyse the current position

The company must appoint someone to take control of the restructuring project. This person, the chief restructuring officer,

"RO" needs to determine the long-term viability of the business and its distinctive service and/or product lines. Tough decisions need to be made, and quickly, on what is viewed as being viable into the future. Within that, the RO needs to understand the legalities surrounding those decisions and the financial implications 'termination' decisions can have.

Once the RO has determined what service and/or product lines are staying, the RO can start to work on the strategy for survival and to develop a preliminary action plan. The plan will focus on what the company is going to do, who is going to do it and what other resources are required to enable that activity. Within that element of the plan, there will be operational, financial, budgeting and legal considerations.

2. Stabilise – focus on immediate needs

The RO needs to focus on immediate survival and also needs to ensure that the rest of the management team understand that this is a crisis situation. The RO needs to raise sufficient cash flow to support the turnaround strategy, particularly at the outset. He or she needs to identify and begin working on securing the necessary future resources.

To stabilise the current crisis, the RO must also secure the support of key stakeholders, such as customers, creditors and employees. Clear communication is key at this early stage, and the RO will have to communicate to the stakeholders the negative impact on them should they choose not to buy in to the restructuring plan. As previously mentioned, if management have reacted early enough, then key stakeholders are inclined to support the turnaround project rather than risk the liquidation of a key supplier/customer.

3. Advocate – implement change

The RO must weed out impediments to change and be an advocate of the restructuring plan. Clearly, management support and stakeholder buy in are vital elements of this advocacy process. A new management team is likely to be required and this will have to be organised by the RO. Clear communication of what is happening, and what the objectives are, is essential to promote advocacy and to keep the turnaround project on track. The RO must meet with key stakeholders, such as key customers and key creditors, and communicate the factors for making the turnaround a success.

4. Reorganise

The RO must set the new strategic direction, focusing on profitable activities and divesting of underperforming projects. The new strategic plan needs to be communicated to the new management team.

5. Improve

The RO must implement process improvement programs and look at supply chain organisation. Cost cutting must be a core element of the turnaround process and it is important to highlight this at the start of a turnaround project. Cost cutting has the dual effect of setting the right tone and ensuring that relevant parties get the clear message that this is a real crisis and that decisive action is required, and is being taken.

As can be seen, the RO is more than just a financial person; the RO's role is effectively the role of a temporary CEO, and it is this closeness in function that can often be an impediment to achieving buy in from the management team/board of directors. However, this resistance must be overcome if the turnaround is to be a success. There must be change, and the change must be radical and delivered in a short time-frame in order to have the necessary impact on the organisation and to demonstrate to key stakeholders that the organisation is tackling its problems decisively and with vigour.

Practical problems with turnaround strategies in Ireland

We have touched on some of these problems previously but, in summary, the most common practical problems with turnaround strategies in Ireland currently are:

- lack of management buy-in or commitment

- reluctance of management to implement tough decisions, because of the intertwined relationships between family members in SME companies

- sales-focused directors of SMEs, who believe that the next big contract will save them

- a current lack of refinance options due to the credit crunch, as both equity and debt markets are stagnant

- directors of Irish SMEs tend to react too late to financial problems, often because they do not have timely financial information to manage the business effectively and, thereby, erode creditor support to such a point that creditors are often unwilling to work with the company anymore

- under Irish legislation, except for the examination process, the Irish tax authorities are precluded from voluntarily writing down a debt. Thus, in a turnaround project in Ireland the tax arrears must be paid in full (albeit that the timing of those payments can be staggered). Unfortunately, SMEs that are in financial difficulty have often been in difficulty for some time and have built up tax liabilities to such a significant level that an informal restructuring or a turnaround project are simply not feasible.

 ## Options other than turnaround

As previously indicated, insolvency practitioners are often faced with the scenario that a turnaround is not going to be feasible and in those circumstances have to look at the more conventional solutions to a corporate insolvency. These conventional solutions have been addressed in detail in the previous chapters of this book, and are:

- creditors' voluntary liquidation

- receivership

- official liquidation/court liquidation

- examinations/schemes of arrangement

As we have already examined the mechanics of the above processes, our intention here is to highlight some **critical points** about each for the professional advisor to keep in mind when talking to his or her client.

We will start with the most common form of formal insolvency: **creditors' voluntary liquidation**.

Going concern and creditors' voluntary liquidations

Although the liquidation process is by its nature not designed to enhance the going concern prospects of a company, a liquidator is not precluded from attempting to preserve some or all of the going concern.

To this end, if a liquidator is appointed to a company that has not ceased to trade and the liquidator believes that there may be an intrinsic value in the business activity, then that liquidator might choose to continue to trade on his own account.

The liquidator would have to ensure that they have the necessary financing and insurance in place to maintain the business activity and this will not be easy to organise at short notice. However, experienced insolvency practitioners will probably have faced such obstacles before and are likely to have access to specialised insolvency insurance policies and banking facilities that would enable them to keep some or all of the company's activities alive.

If this is feasible, then the liquidator will be in a position to advertise the business and assets as a going concern, albeit in liquidation. In such a scenario, it is not the company that is for sale, but rather its business and assets. Under such circumstances, a competitor may be interested in acquiring those assets in order to expand their own business.

The incumbent directors are not automatically precluded from acquiring those assets, but such a sale would require a statutory notice to the creditors and, where a committee of inspection has been formed, it would be preferable that the sale be approved by the committee of inspection.

By maintaining the going concern, the liquidator is improving the asset realisations, not alone by achieving a value for the going concern, but also in that such a sale would often encompass the tangible assets of the company and as such are likely to achieve a better price when sold as part of a going concern. Furthermore, debtor realisations are often also improved, as customers of the insolvent entity experience less disruption to their service and have less reason not to pay.

Court liquidation

I n certain situations, directors can find themselves in a position where they have concerns over their ability to preserve the assets of the company for the benefit of the general body of creditors, until such time as the liquidator is appointed, which in the case

of a creditors' voluntary liquidation has an associated minimum 10-day notice period.

In such circumstances, the directors might consider making an application to the High Court for the immediate appointment of a liquidator, **thereby securing the assets for the general body of creditors**. The circumstances of each case may be unique, but for accountants whose clients find themselves in an impossible position and in need of urgent action it is an option that can and should be considered.

There are no additional implications for the directors in respect of their "honest and responsible behaviour" and the liquidator will file his report in that regard with the ODCE, as is done in creditors' voluntary liquidations.

As in a creditors' voluntary liquidation, the directors must prepare a statement of affairs, but in this instance the format is more detailed and is a sworn statement that is presented to the High Court at a date which is set by the High Court.

It is important to note that there is likely to be a **greater cost** associated with the court liquidation process and it would not normally be suitable for the liquidation of a small company.

Examination

W here a company has a **reasonable prospect of survival**, examination may be an option. However, a reasonable prospect of survival alone is not sufficient; the company must also be capable of generating sufficient cash flow to operate for the full period of protection, and of attracting a sufficient injection of capital to achieve a compromise with the creditors and cover the costs of the examination.

Clients are obviously inclined to prefer the examination option over any other form of insolvency procedure, as the process is designed to maintain the going concern and to restructure the liabilities of the company, so as to enable the company to continue to trade as normal once the examination has been successfully completed.

In practice, the difficulty we are faced with as the professional advisors is distinguishing between a client that actually has a reasonable prospect of survival and one where the client, because of their obvious vested interests, believes through hope rather than fact, that the company has a reasonable prospect of survival.

Clearly, this is a very difficult decision for both the directors and their advisors. Livelihoods are at stake, not just in the immediate client company, but also possibly in the creditor entities caught in the insolvency. Recently, the Irish courts have intimated their dissatisfaction with the frequency of unsuccessful examinations and have begun to strenuously question the opinions proffered in the independent accountant's report.

This view of the Irish Courts makes what is a difficult report for the independent accountant, all the more difficult. However, these Court rulings will assist advisors in demonstrating to clients that pursuing an examination is not an easy option and that it is increasingly difficult to obtain the protection of the High Court for the purpose of an examination.

Currently, with a critical shortage of debt and equity funds, achieving a successful examination is proving all the more difficult.

Companies may be in a position to generate positive cash flow for the protection period, but what are the prospects of there being a willing investor who has the ability to generate sufficient capital?

At the time of writing, it is unclear whether the establishment of the National Asset Management Agency (NAMA) will be successful in commencing the flow of credit from Irish banks. Hopefully, however, as the effects of the current credit crunch subside, the ability of such companies to attract capital investment will improve, leading to more successful examinations. With more successful examinations, we believe that there will be more debate on the issue of competing creditor rights, and we anticipate some interesting judgments from the Irish courts on the matter.

In particular, the subject of the rights of secured creditors in examinations has the potential to be contentious. Given the current property slump, many loans are secured on property whose value has fallen substantially below the level of the associated debt, and the following questions arise:

- Is an Irish Court going to force a secured lender to take a write down in an examination (often referred to as 'the Cram Down') based on current market valuations? **or, alternatively,**

- will the Court allow the payment of dividends to preferential and unsecured creditors at a reduced level to effectively finance the shortfall in sums due to a secured lender where the borrowings are higher than the value of the secured assets?

Only time will tell.

When considering corporate recovery options with clients, examination is going to be high on the list. However, it is not suited to all companies, and given the recent soundings from the Irish courts, it is going to be harder to achieve than in the past.

 ## Receivership

Compared to other insolvency procedures, directors are less involved in the receivership process. Although directors sometimes invite the charge holder to appoint a receiver, once the process has commenced the receiver usually takes full control of the company and its associated issues.

As discussed in **Chapter 3**, the receiver acts on behalf of the charge holder and his or her objective is to maximise the return to the charge holder. To this end a receiver will often attempt to continue to trade and to offer the business and assets for sale as a going concern, in order to enhance asset values.

Unlike an examination, the assets of the company are sold and, ultimately, the directors have the responsibility to dissolve the insolvent company when the receivership is complete. Normally, this would be achieved through a creditors' voluntary liquidation.

When advising clients in a receivership, it is important to encourage them to work with and assist the receiver in their role. At the outset, the directors will be obliged to file a statement of affairs and the directors should do their upmost to file the statement of affairs within the allotted time. It is often in the directors' personal interests to work with a receiver. They are often exposed under personal guarantees to the secured lender, so

achieving the best price possible for the assets is in the mutual interest of the secured lender and the guarantor.

As with the examination process, a receiver does not have a statutory obligation to file a report with the ODCE on the honest and responsible behaviour of the directors. However, a receiver does have authority to take legal action against directors or officers of the company where he believes there may have been a fraud perpetrated or a case of reckless trading. A receiver may also consider the appropriateness of taking restriction or disqualification proceedings against directors under section 150 or section 160 CA 1990.

 ## Matters that can give rise to litigation

Fraudulent preference – material payment to selective or connected creditors

Professional advisors should ensure that their clients are aware of the dangers of a fraudulent preference payment.

Such a circumstance might typically arise where directors of an insolvent company lodge debtor funds into a company bank account that is overdrawn and personally guaranteed, while they knew or ought to have known that their company was insolvent/unable to pay its debts as they fell due.

In such circumstances, the position of the directors has been improved because their exposure under the personal guarantee to the bank has been reduced. If, within a short period of time, the company was to enter into liquidation, and if that transaction was material in amount, it is likely that a liquidator will spot the transaction and consider it to be a fraudulent preference within the meaning of section 286 CA 1963.

Similar circumstances might appear where directors have given personal guarantees to large suppliers.

In addition, apart from personal guarantees, if a director is seen to simply prefer particular creditors or a creditor over others at a time when he knew or ought to have known that the company was insolvent, then questions are going to arise as to the honest and responsible behaviour of those directors in the context of the liquidator's report to the ODCE pursuant to section 56 CLEA 2001.

It is also worth bearing in mind that such payments to connected parties are reversible for a period of up to two years preceding the date of liquidation.

 Case Study –
Re Frederick Inns
Limited (1999)

By way of example of a reported fraudulent preference, one could consider the case of *Re Frederick Inns Limited* (1999). In that case, there were nine companies in a group, which was indebted to the Revenue Commissioners for a total of IR£2.8 million (€3.5 million). In light of such a large debt the Revenue had threatened the company with a winding up petition. In reaction, the directors agreed that the assets of three of the companies be sold and that the proceeds of the sale be applied to discharge the debts of the whole group.

Subsequently, the companies were wound up, including the three companies whose assets were sold. A liquidator was appointed and that liquidator issued proceedings for the recovery of the said proceeds of sale insofar as they had been applied against the indebtedness of other group companies.

The court held that the payments were voluntary payments without consideration and that they were made at a time when the companies in question were insolvent. The liquidator succeeded in his claim. The judgment stated that "the payments were misapplications of the respective companies' assets because they were made when the companies were insolvent and the payments were in disregard of the rights and interests of the general creditors".

Continuing to trade while insolvent

The clearest definition of insolvency is **when a company is unable to pay its debts as they fall due**. There is, of course, the situation where a company is insolvent as per its balance sheet at a particular point in time, but that definition can be clouded by the specific nature of the items in that balance sheet. However, there are significant dangers for directors in continuing to trade while they knew, or ought to have known, that their company was insolvent, and there are many options open to a receiver or liquidator, if appointed, to pursue the directors for their actions.

It is a basic requirement of responsible behaviour for directors that they maintain proper books and records, and are aware of the financial position of their company. Failure to maintain such financial controls is likely to be deemed irresponsible, and is likely to lead to those directors facing a restriction application in the High Court. Where those financial controls are in place, but the directors choose to ignore the insolvent position of the company, and blindly continue to trade, they are also likely to face restriction proceedings in the High Court.

Directors have a duty of care to the creditors, and as such should be managing the company in such a way as to mitigate the losses for the general body of creditors. With this in mind, while the directors are not precluded from attempting to trade out of the difficulties, they need to be mindful of corporate governance and should formally record their decisions and the reasons for those decisions through formal board minutes. Although they may be going through stressful and turbulent times, it is important that the directors formally record their decisions because, if they were to fail in their attempts to keep the company 'alive', it is likely that they will be asked to explain their recovery strategy to a liquidator as part of the liquidator's reporting process to the ODCE.

In relation to board minutes, it is also important to note that the liquidator's report to the ODCE includes all directors who were directors in the 12 months preceding the commencement of the liquidation. With that in mind, it is important that any director who is resigning his directorship from a company ensures that their resignation is filed with the CRO in a timely manner.

Fraudulent Trading

Section 297 CA 1963 states that:

> "where a person is knowingly a party to the carrying on of a business with intent to defraud creditors of the company, or creditors of any other person or for any fraudulent purpose, that person shall be guilty of an offence".

If a person is found guilty, there is a maximum penalty of up to seven years imprisonment and/or a fine not exceeding €63,487. Furthermore, that person can also be held personally liable, without limitation, for all or any part of the debts or other liabilities of the company as the court may direct.

Despite what might be alleged at a typical meeting of creditors, it is evident from the above penalties that the courts do not take the allegation of fraudulent trading lightly; there is, therefore, a high bar to be overcome in proving such an allegation. To date, there have not been many such cases in the courts; for further reference, the following cases are of note:

- *Re Kelly's Carpetdrome Limited* **(1983)**
  The destruction of records and illegal transfer of assets

- *Aluminium Fabricators Limited* **(1984)**
  The keeping of two sets of records for the purposes of providing false information to auditors and creditors

- *Hunting Lodges Limited* **(1985)**
  Misappropriation of funds arising from the sale of a company asset

- *Contract Packaging Limited* **(1992)**
  Fraudulent misappropriation of company funds through personal bank accounts

- *Eastland Warehousing Limited* **(1999)**
  Fraudulent misappropriation of excise duties and taxes collected on behalf of the tax authorities

- *Doherty Advertising Limited* **(2004)**
  Fraudulent raising of bank finance through the creation of false invoices in an invoice discounting agreement.

The important point to note is that in proving such a case the applicant must demonstrate **fraudulent intent** on the part of the directors, which is not easy to prove. Directors should be aware, however, of the very serious penalties that would arise if a case of fraudulent trading is proven against them.

Reckless Trading

Alongside fraudulent trading in the Companies Act 1963, one will find reckless trading at section 297(A). This section was subsequently amended by the Companies Act 1990 (CA 1990) and now provides that personal liability can be imposed on the directors of a company where such a person was "knowingly a party to the carrying on of any business of the company in a reckless manner".

The Act gives two specific circumstances that would be deemed reckless:

1] where a person was a party to the carrying on of the business and, having regard to the general knowledge, skill and experience that may reasonably be expected of a person in his position, he ought to have known that his actions or those of the company would cause loss to the creditors of the company

2] where a person was a party to the contracting of a debt by the company and did not honestly believe on reasonable grounds that the company would be able to pay the debt when it fell due for payment as well as all its other debts (taking into account the contingent and prospective liabilities).

In practice, directors should take note of point 2 above, as it raises very serious concerns for directors of companies that are experiencing financial difficulty. Section 297A also contains a defence to the effect that where a person has acted honestly and responsibly in relation to the conduct of the affairs of the company, the court may relieve him or her wholly, or in parts from personal liability.

As with fraudulent trading, a case of reckless trading against a director is a very serious matter, which carries the prospect of personal liability. Directors and their professional advisors should be very cognisant of point 2 above. The case of *Re Hefferon Kearns* (1993) remains the leading Irish decision as regards reckless trading.

Failure to keep proper books of account

Section 202 CA 1990 requires every company to keep proper books of account. In summary, the books should correctly record and explain the transactions of the company and enable, at any time, the financial position to be determined with reasonable accuracy.

The books should also be maintained on a continuous and consistent basis, and the entries made in a timely manner and be consistent from one year to the next.

The books should record monies received and expended, as well as the assets and liabilities of the company. Ultimately, the books of account should give a true and fair view of the state of affairs of the company and explain the transactions into which it has entered.

The liability of officers of the company in this regard is defined at sections 203 and 204 CA 1990. The penalties for failing to keep proper books of account include maximum fines up to €12,697, and there is also a risk of personal liability for officers of the company where the company

becomes insolvent and is being wound up.

In this regard, "if the court considers that such contravention has contributed to the company's inability to pay all of its debts or has resulted in substantial uncertainty as to the assets and liabilities of the company or has substantially impeded the orderly winding up thereof, the court on the application of the liquidator or any creditor or contributory" can make the officers of the company personally liable without limitation for all or part of the debts of the company.

The above factors are clearly pertinent to the question of restriction and disqualification under section 150 and section 160 CA, which was discussed above in **Chapter 7**.

Conclusion

The importance to directors, in the performance of their duties, of reliable financial information produced in a timely manner cannot be overstated.

Too often it is our experience as insolvency practitioners that, if directors had been aware at an earlier stage of the severity of their financial losses, significant additional losses to creditors may have been prevented and in many cases a formal restructuring program implemented, helping to preserve some or all of the business.

Clearly, in the absence of reliable and timely financial information, directors are not going to be in a position to react to their financial problems until it is too late.

However, where directors have the foresight to insist on reliable and timely financial information, they will be in a position to be alerted by the early warning signs enabling them to take corrective action at the appropriate time.

Early action is paramount. It increases the chances of survival, enhances asset values and enables the correction to be consensual rather than enforced.

Unfortunately, human emotions come in to play (denial and hope in particular), which delay the effective response that is needed from management, leading to the unwanted situation of enforced change. If only we would learn from the mistakes of others; there are plenty of examples to choose from.

Relevant Parties

Chapter 9 Overview

>> Introduction

>> Bankers

>> Committee of Inspection

>> Company's auditors/accountants

>> Companies Registration Office

>> Trade Creditors

>> Department of Enterprise, Trade and Employment

>> Department of Social and Family Affairs

>> Directors

>> Employees

>> The High Court

>> Insurers and Insurance Brokers

>> Lease and Hire Purchase Financiers

>> Legal advisors

>> Office of the Director of Corporate Enforcement

>> Office of the High Court Examiner

>> The Revenue Commissioners

>> Shareholders

Introduction

There are many different parties involved at different levels in the progress of an insolvency in Ireland. Outlined below are the main interested parties, their respective roles and an overview table showing whether the party has any role in a particular insolvency assignment.

RELEVANT PARTY	Creditors' Voluntary Liquidation	Court Liquidation	Receivership	Examination	Members' Voluntary Liquidation
Bankers / Financiers	Y	Y	Y	Y	Y/N
Committee of Inspection	Y/N	Y/N	Y	Y/N	Y
Company's Auditors / Accountants	Y	Y	Y	Y	Y
Companies Registration Office	Y	Y	Y	Y	Y
Creditors	Y	Y	Y	Y	Y/N
Department of Enterprise, Trade and Employment	Y	Y	Y	Y/N	Y/N
Dept. of Social and Family Affairs	Y	Y	Y	N	N
Directors	Y	Y	Y	Y	Y
Employees	Y	Y	Y	Y	N
High Court	N	Y	N	Y	N
Insurers	Y	Y	Y	Y	Y/N
Legal Advisors	Y	Y	Y	Y	Y/N
Office of the Director of Corporate Enforcement	Y	Y	N	N	N
Office of the High Court Examiner	Y	Y	N	Y	N
Revenue Commissioners	Y	Y	Y	Y	Y
Shareholders	Y	Y	Y/N	Y	Y

▶▶ Bankers

In any type of liquidation or receivership, an insolvency practitioner should contact the company's bankers on appointment to ascertain the extent of any assets available and ensure that no further payments are made from the company's accounts.

The company's bankers are often creditors of the company and, like other creditors, need to be informed of the progress of the insolvency and the prospects of a recovery of part or all of the sums owing (payments in this regard are referred to as *dividends*).

A key element of an insolvency practitioner's investigations into the affairs of an insolvent company is a review of the company's bank accounts, and it is important that a practitioner ensures that all bank statements and correspondence with the bank are available as early as possible into the insolvency. To this end, the company's bankers are an important source of information.

In an examination, it may be necessary to obtain agreement from the bank to use secured assets to continue to trade (such as debtors subject to invoice discounting) so immediate and regular contact with the company's bankers is of high importance.

The bank's role in a receivership is dealt with in detail in **Chapter 3**.

During a members' voluntary liquidation, the company's bankers have often already been paid in full or will be paid in full. As a result, their involvement is usually minimal.

▶▶ Committee of Inspection

A committee of inspection is a representative body of members and creditors. The role of the committee is as follows:

- liaise with the company's creditors on behalf of the liquidator

- provide the liquidator with information on the company's activities

- aid the liquidator in the investigation of the company's affairs

- approve fees

- approve legal actions

- attend meetings to review the course of the liquidation.

Usually, the committee of inspection will be issued a letter by the practitioner on appointment and meetings/updates are held or issued as needed during the course of the insolvency.

A committee of inspection can be appointed in a court liquidation, an examination or a creditors' voluntary liquidation.

Company's auditors / accountants

The company's auditor/accountant is often the referrer of the insolvency project, and it is important for any insolvency practitioner to keep the company's auditor/accountant up-to-date with:

● the main issues in the case,

● the progress of the investigation (where possible), and

● the eventual outcome of the case.

The company's auditor/accountant is an important source of information about the company's assets, trading and history. Furthermore, they are often better placed than the insolvency practitioner to prepare outstanding tax returns or financial figures, which can result in a substantial cost saving.

Often in court liquidations or receiverships, the company's auditor is called upon to prepare the statement of affairs after the commencement of the insolvency. Similarly, the company's auditor usually prepares the declaration of solvency in a members' voluntary liquidation.

Before an examination, the company's auditor/accountant often prepares the independent accountant's report (albeit that recent High Court rulings may result in this report being completed, in future, by accountants with a specific insolvency background) on which the examiner will report to both the High Court and the creditors. Again, the importance of contact with the company's auditor/accountant is evident so that the insolvency practitioner fully understands the basis of the accountant's opinions in the independent accountant's report and can accurately report on same.

In summary, the role of the company's auditor/accountant in a court liquidation, a creditors' voluntary liquidation, or a receivership, is as follows:

▪ to provide the insolvency practitioner with copies of the company's financial statements or accounts

▪ to provide the practitioner with information on the company's assets, activities, directors and related parties

▪ to aid the liquidator in the investigation of the company's affairs.

It is of note that an auditor or accountant who fails to provide information to an appointed liquidator, examiner or receiver can be compelled to do so by order of the High Court. Significant cost implications can arise, as can disciplinary action from respective accounting bodies for any auditor or accountant who fails to deliver up information to which the insolvency practitioner is entitled.

Companies Registration Office (CRO)

The Companies Registration Office supervises the filing of the statutory return obligations for any liquidation, receivership or examination. Though the forms to be filed and information they require are straightforward, it should be noted that failure to comply with statutory returns is both a civil and criminal offence.

The CRO is also a significant source of information, as it will enable details and information to be obtained on related companies, debtors and creditors.

Trade Creditors

Obviously, a creditor's main interest in any insolvency is to recover as much of the funds due to them as possible. From this point of view, it is important to notify the creditors of dividend prospects as early as possible.

A receiver has no obligation under statute to unsecured trade creditors and in a liquidation (other than court liquidations) obligations predominantly extend to holding annual meetings. However, it is best practice to keep creditors notified of the progress of the insolvency as follows:

- advise creditors of the insolvency and the appointment of the insolvency practitioner as early as possible, thereafter

- notify creditors of the likely outcome of the case as regards the investigation of the company's affairs and dividend prospects

- hold meetings as specified in the Companies Acts 1963–2009

- deal with creditors' queries or claims in a timely and professional manner.

Of note, also, is that, in the absence of a committee of inspection, the creditors of the company ultimately approve fees in a creditors' voluntary liquidation.

Department of Enterprise, Trade and Employment (DETE)

Many years ago legislation was enacted to set up an insolvency fund to safeguard the employees of insolvent employers. This fund is administered by the DETE and, in terms of insolvencies, the DETE is divided into two main sections:

The Insolvency Section

In brief, the Insolvency Section processes the claims of any employee or non-proprietary director of the company (usually a director with less than a 15% shareholding in the company) in respect of:

- arrears of wages

- holiday pay

- minimum notice

- pensions

- certain deductions

- awards from the Labour Court

- decisions by the Rights Commissioners

The Redundancy Section

The Redundancy Section of the DETE processes redundancy claims, both in respect of redundancies by:

- solvent companies, whereby it processes a 60% rebate for the employer of the statutory amount paid, and

- insolvent companies, whereby it processes the entire statutory redundancy claim for the employee and submits a claim for the sum paid less the 60% rebate in the liquidation.

The DETE usually takes the place of the employee as a preferential creditor for the sums paid to employees on behalf of the company, albeit that the Insolvency Section can under certain circumstances pay out more to an employee for arrears of wages than is allowable as a preferential claim.

The processing of employee claims is a substantial task, and it takes several weeks, and sometimes months, for claims to be paid. To facilitate the DETE and expedite payments to employees, employee claims should not be submitted to the DETE in drip-feed fashion and all claim forms of the insolvent company should be furnished at one time to the extent possible with all supporting information and detail.

It is important to note that the Insolvency Section will not process employee claims **during an examination** and, therefore, the company in examination must bear the cost directly. For cash flow purposes, the sum due to the employee can be placed in the scheme as a creditor to be paid in line with the DETE limits.

The Redundancy Section of the DETE will make a payment during the course of an examination (as it can, even when an insolvent company has not entered an insolvency arrangement) and can be included in the scheme for the amount paid out, less the 60% rebate.

(The DETE has a very detailed and informative Website: **www.entemp.ie**)

Department of Social and Family Affairs (DSFA)

The DSFA often become involved with insolvent companies before a liquidation or receivership has even occurred, as often, on being made redundant, employees will automatically go to the nearest DSFA office for the purpose of claiming unemployment entitlements or "signing on".

Despite the fact that they are often not formally appointed at this stage, insolvency practitioners should ensure that the director/directors of the company pass the following documents to the employee on the termination of their employment and thereby ensure that the former employee's claims for social assistance are not delayed:

- Form P45

- Statement of levy deductions

- Form RP50

- Letter of termination

While certain DSFA offices may allow former employees to "sign on" without all of these documents, having the above should guarantee that no delays occur.

In terms of ongoing insolvencies, the DSFA are often the silent partner of the DETE as follows:

- employee claims are checked against the records of the DSFA by the DETE to confirm that the employee was not making any form of social welfare claim while in employment

- the DFSA's Scope Section will examine and determine the suitability of any director or shareholder of a company to have a claim processed through the DETE

If the company has been compliant with the filing of its PAYE and PRSI returns, the role of the DSFA can be quite nominal in the course of an insolvency. As an insolvency practitioner or accountant/ auditor dealing with or advising an insolvent company, it is strongly advised that you ensure that the company's P35 returns are all filed; this should mean that you may never have to deal with the DSFA, as the records they need to review claims for any form of social assistance are readily available.

 **Directors**

Of course, the company's directors are involved in the insolvency of every company and will have an involvement during most, if not all of the process.

In summary, the role of the company's directors during a court liquidation, a creditors' voluntary liquidation or receivership is as follows:

- deliver up the assets of the company to the insolvency practitioner

- deliver the pertinent books and records of the company to the insolvency practitioner

- provide the practitioner with information on the company's assets, activities, directors and related parties

- aid the liquidator in the investigation of the company's affairs.

The obligation on directors to assist a liquidator is somewhat at odds with the obligation on a liquidator appointed in a court or creditors' voluntary liquidation under section 56 of the Company Law Enforcement Act 2001 (CLEA 2001) to bring a restriction application against the same directors.

In any insolvency, it is important that the directors are treated in a fair manner and are kept up-to-date with:

- the main issues in the case,

- the progress of the investigation (where possible), and

- the eventual outcome of the case.

During an examination, the role of the directors usually remains unchanged in that they continue to control the company and act in the same roles and manner and with the same rights, obligations and duties as before the examination.

 Employees

Much of the involvement of employees during the course of an insolvency is outlined in the above sections concerning the Department of Enterprise, Trade and Employment and the Department of Social and Family Affairs. It is rare for employees to be involved in a members' voluntary liquidation, as they would usually be paid in full at the time that the company's trade ceased.

It is important for any accountant, be they internal to the company, an external auditor or insolvency practitioner, to remember that employees are often the most severely impacted upon by the insolvency of a company, and that those employees with long periods of service can be very substantial creditors of the company.

It is important to ensure that:

- the correct forms and paperwork are given to the employees on termination

- mortgage protection forms are actively sought out and prepared

- unions are kept fully informed of the status of their members' claims

- employees are contacted or met with as early as possible so that they are fully briefed on the process and claims prepared expeditiously

- funds, once paid by the DETE, are paid to the employee without delay.

 The High Court

The High Court has an extensive role in insolvencies in Ireland.

In a **court liquidation**, the High Court monitors the progress and outcome of the liquidation and the actions of the liquidator. The High Court also approves the costs and expenses of the provisional and/or official liquidator.

In an **examination**, the High Court again monitors the progress and outcome of the case and the actions of the examiner and the company in examination. Ultimate approval of any scheme of arrangement prepared and approved by the company's creditors rests with the High Court. The High Court also has a key role in the approval of the costs of the examination, especially in cases where the examination has been unsuccessful.

In a **creditors' voluntary liquidation**, all restriction applications pursuant to section 150 of the Companies Act 1990 (CA 1990) are heard by the High Court, as are any applications for relief from restriction under section 152 CA 1990. Furthermore, it is open to any liquidator to seek directions from the High Court on complex areas lacking clarity or matters of significant importance.

The High Court would not have an automatic role in most **members' voluntary liquidations** or **receiverships** (unless it is a court-appointed receivership).

Again, however, it is open for the liquidator of a company in members' voluntary liquidation or receiver to seek the directions of the court. It is also open to a receiver to bring restriction, disqualification or other substantive proceedings, which would fall under the jurisdiction of the High Court.

Insurers and Insurance Brokers

In any type of liquidation or receivership, an insolvency practitioner should contact the company's insurers (usually through the company's brokers) on appointment to ascertain whether the company's insurance is in place and to determine:

- details of all policies held by the company and whether same remain in place

- details of any potential refunds due to the company

- details of any claims for or against the company

- details of the assets insured by the company

Continuing the company's own insurance (often referred to as "piggybacking") is often very cost efficient. However, it useful to note that **many insurance policies cancel immediately on the appointment of a liquidator, receiver or examiner** (even if paid up-to-date) and this can have very significant impact on post-appointment intentions.

In circumstances where it has not proved possible to continue the company's own insurance, there are now a number of

insurance brokers offering specialised insolvency insurance cover to insolvency practitioners. However, the most comprehensive cover and policies remain those offered by insurance brokers who have supplied insolvency insurance over the last number of years.

Finally, it should be noted that professional indemnity insolvency insurance for a practitioner is effectively a pre-requisite to acting in any role appointed by the High Court.

Lease and Hire Purchase Financiers

On the insolvency of a company, such financiers' immediate concern relates to the location and security of their assets. Any accountant advising a company should endeavour to make the appointed insolvency practitioner aware of the existence of leased assets as early as possible to ensure that:

- the assets are secured as soon as possible

- the exposure to personal guarantees of the signatories to the finance lease or HP agreement is not exacerbated

Once located and secure, insolvency practitioners should endeavour to have the assets valued and determine whether there would be any funds available from the sale of these assets over and above the finance liabilities thereon (usually referred to as equity) for the benefit of the company's creditors on the sale of the assets. Once it is clear that equity is not available, the financed assets should be returned to the finance company as soon as possible. If equity is available, the insolvency practitioner should advise the finance company of the intention to settle the agreement as early as possible and then pay the outstanding finance liability without undue delay.

In an examination, agreement should be obtained for the continued use of leased or hire purchase equipment.

In any type of liquidation or receivership, an insolvency practitioner should contact the company's lease and hire purchase financiers on appointment to ascertain the extent of any assets available and ensure that no further payments are made from the company's accounts.

The company's lease and hire purchase financiers often remain creditors of the company even after disposal of the assets subject to finance and like other creditors need to be informed of the progress of the insolvency and dividend prospects.

There are three points of note with regard to assets subject to such lease or hire purchase agreements:

- care must be taken in returning a financed asset where there may be a retention of title claim over a part of same (e.g. tyres on a leased vehicle)

- insurance or sales proceeds obtained by the company or an insolvency practitioner in respect of a financed asset is payable to the finance company involved up to the value of the liability on the agreement

- In circumstances where a lease/hire purchase financier has many agreements in place with a company,

certain agreements provide for any equity arising under one lease agreement to be offset against deficit or shortfalls arising in other agreements

During a members' voluntary liquidation, the company's financiers have often already been paid in full or will be paid in full. As a result, their involvement is usually minimal.

 Legal Advisors

Like the company's auditor/accountant, the company's legal advisor is often the referrer of the insolvency project, and it is important for any insolvency practitioner to keep the company's legal advisor up-to-date with:

- the main issues in the case,

- the progress of the investigation (where possible), and

- the eventual outcome of the case.

The company's legal advisor is often an important source of information about the company's trading and history and in any type of insolvency, the company's legal advisors should be contacted by the insolvency practitioner on their appointment to determine

- details of all proceedings brought by the company

- details of all proceedings brought against the company.

Details of all outstanding litigation against the company is a matter for inclusion in a report pursuant to section 56 CLEA 2001.

As with other professional advisors who fail to provide information to an appointed liquidator, examiner or receiver, legal advisors can be compelled to do so by order of the High Court. Significant cost implications can arise as a result of the making of an order to compel a solicitor to hand over such information, as can disciplinary action from the Law Society of Ireland.

Insolvency often leads to confrontational situations for insolvency practitioners whether it be with disputed debtors, irate landlords, disgruntled creditors or errant directors. Practical, commercial and cost effective legal advice is invaluable to any insolvency practitioner.

Office of the Director of Corporate Enforcement (ODCE)

The ODCE and its role in Irish insolvency are extensively discussed in **Chapter 7**.

The ODCE is the overseeing body for insolvency in Ireland and the following is important:

- the **immediate** notification of the ODCE on the appointment of a liquidator by way of a creditors' voluntary liquidation or court liquidation

- the timely filing of detailed, accurate and balanced reports pursuant to section 56 CLEA 2001

- that queries raised by the ODCE are finalised without delay

- the timely outcome of any proceedings brought against directors

- the timely notification of the closing of any case.

Office of the High Court Examiner

A detailed account of the role of the Examiner and his staff is included in **Chapter 4**.

The Office is concerned with the following:

- court-related company law matters

- bankruptcy matters

- administration and mortgage suits

In simple terms, the Office of the High Court Examiner is the civil service support for the court system when dealing with insolvencies. However, it is important to note that a sitting before the Examiner and/or an Assistant Examiner is a sitting before the High Court and appropriate deference should be paid accordingly.

The Revenue Commissioners

In outline, the role of the Revenue Commissioners is to ensure compliance with the relevant tax Acts in terms of both the filing of tax returns and the payment of taxes.

The filing of tax returns

The main reasons that any insolvency practitioner or accountant advising a company should seek to complete the company's outstanding tax returns are as follows:

- to ascertain the super preferential, preferential and unsecured claims of the Revenue Commissioners

- to ensure that the PRSI/social welfare record of employees is complete

- to confirm the detail necessary for inclusion in response to Question 20 of the liquidator's report pursuant to section 56 CLEA 2001

- In particular, the failure to complete a pre-liquidation P35 can have a very detrimental impact on employees if they seek to claim any form of social welfare payment including unemployment benefit and assistance, dental and medical benefits and state pension.

For the reasons outlined above, the Revenue Commissioners will invariably seek the completion of the company's tax returns be the company in **receivership** or **liquidation**.

In an **examination**, the completion of the company's tax returns is necessary for the proper calculation of the company's tax liabilities for inclusion in the scheme of arrangement.

In a **members' voluntary liquidation**, all tax returns must be completed, filed and paid, or the Revenue Commissioners will be unable to give clearance for the finalisation of the liquidation.

The payment of taxes

In all aspects of insolvency, the role of the Revenue Commissioners is to maximise the return to the State exchequer by way of dividends, relevant contract tax certificates received or redundancy rebate offsets.

In circumstances where the State is at a significant loss as a result of the actions of the directors of a company, the Revenue Commissioners tend to be vocal regarding the honesty and responsibility and in many cases have provided the necessary funding and/or support to pursue company directors through the courts to make them liable for all or part of the company's deficit.

Other specific roles of the Revenue Commissioners

The Revenue Commissioners can also be an excellent source of information on the company's trading and the manner in which it handled its tax affairs.

In **creditors' voluntary liquidations**, the Revenue Commissioners are often the largest creditor and therefore may control the vote for the appointment of a liquidator at any meeting of creditors.

In **receiverships**, the role of the Revenue Commissioners may not be as significant in cases where the receiver is appointed by a way of a fixed charge/debenture.

In **court liquidations**, the Revenue Commissioners will often be notice parties to proceedings or applications brought by the official liquidator.

In **examinations**, the Revenue
Commissioners are again often notice
parties, and the High Court will often seek
the views of the Revenue Commissioners
in respect of the proposals set down for
approval by the Court

 ## Shareholders

The majority of companies in Ireland
are owner-operated and, as a result,
the directors and shareholders are usually
one and the same.

Unfortunately, in any form of insolvency,
the shareholders are last in line for
recovery, and it is rare that the
shareholders would obtain any recovery
from a company in receivership, or a
company subject to a creditors' voluntary
or court liquidation. As a result, it is
unusual for the shareholders to have an
involvement during the course of such an
insolvency. However, it is advisable for
any insolvency practitioner to make the
shareholders of the company aware of
their appointment as:

● The shareholders may have
   information regarding the actions of
   the company and its directors

● There may be significant financial
   implications for shareholders as a
   result of the loss of their investment

● There are potential tax implications
   arising on capital losses arising on the
   loss of their investment

Shareholders may have a more active
involvement in an examination as the
company would hopefully continue to
trade. In the context of an examination, it
is important to note, the High Court will
not compel the cancellation of a
shareholder's shares.

In a **members' voluntary liquidation**, the
company has sufficient funds to discharge
its liabilities and, therefore, all remaining
funds are distributable amongst the
shareholders. ■